MW01001698

History and the Human Condition

History and the Human Condition

A Historian's Pursuit of Knowledge

John Lukacs

Wilmington, Delaware

Library of Congress Cataloging-in-Publication Data

Lukacs, John, 1924–
History and the human condition : a historian's pursuit of knowledge / John Lukacs.
p. cm.
Includes bibliographical references and index.
ISBN 978-1-61017-065-9 (hardback)
1. History—Philosophy. 2. Historiography—Philosophy. 3. History, Modern—19th century. 4. History, Modern—20th century. I. Title.
D16.8.L825 2012
901—dc23
2011052635

Published in the United States by:

ISI Books
Intercollegiate Studies Institute
3901 Centerville Road
Wilmington, Delaware 19807-1938
www.isibooks.org

Manufactured in the United States of America

This book is dedicated to my dear friends
Evan and Klaus,
and to their wives

Contents

Preface

TO INTRODUCE, OR PREFACE, one's published writing must be easy. But I find it difficult, since such an explanation (Disraeli: "Never complain, never explain") could sound as an apologia. That I certainly wish to avoid. But I think I need to attempt a few sentences to sum up a reason for this book.

History and the Human Condition contains some of my work published during the past ten years, 2002 to 2012. I have had a fairly large writing and publishing career till now. A recurring theme of the more than thirty books and the many hundreds of articles, essays, and reviews I wrote and then published during two-thirds of a century, 1947 to 2002, has been that history is more than the "recorded past," that its study and writing are more than a "science." *Remembered Past: John Lukacs on History, Historians, and Historical Knowledge* was the title of the massive and impressive volume that ISI Books published in 2005. A large book, 923 pages, containing, among other things, a 50-page bibliography, listing about 99 percent of all my published writings from 1947 to 2002. The present book, of course, is smaller in size. It is in some ways a continuation of *Remembered Past* . . . but it is also different in its purpose and its contents. When *Remembered Past* was completed, I was eighty years old and in good health. When *History and the Human Condition* is published, I will be in my ninetieth year, and failing in my strength, inclined to think that I shall no longer write another entire book. During the past ten years I was still blessed with enough physical and mental health to write an estimable amount: a list of my published books from 2002 to 2012 (though not of my articles, essays, and other published writings) may be found at the end of this volume. Selections from my published writings of these past ten years are the contents of this, smaller, volume. But there is also another difference. It is a gradual shift in the emphasis of my principal concerns. This shift, contra Disraeli, may call for an explanation.

From his early years, this ambitious historian has had two different (though not unrelated) interests and concerns. One was my ambition to write history perhaps exceptionally well, but also including themes and contents unlike those that concerned perhaps the majority of academic historians—much of this ambition springing from my conviction that history, its research and then inevitably its writing, was a form of literature rather than "science." The other was my gradual realization not only that historical evidence differs from scientific or legal evidence but also that what a few physicists (Heisenberg rather than Einstein) learned about subatomic matters corresponded amazingly to my own, slow, and often painful realization that both the research and the writing of history (indeed of any portion of a past) has its unavoidable limitations, and that the recognition of this does not impoverish but potentially enriches our minds. I put this in a summary phrase, relevant not just to historical but to all human knowledge: that there is an inevitable relationship between the knower and the known. They are *not* identical, but they *are* inseparable.

Readers of this book may recognize that many of its contents deal with questions about historical knowledge, and perhaps somewhat fewer with historical narratives. Yet many of my recent books contain chapters and arguments of both kinds. They have been results of my preoccupation with historical problems even more than with historical periods. At the same time, many of them illustrate my conviction that an entire great historical period is now over—something that in my earlier writings I had named the Bourgeois Age, the great passage of about five hundred years, from an aristocratic to the beginnings of democratic rule, but that now I prefer to name the European Age. In any case the history of the past five hundred years was suffused with the rise of a historical consciousness appearing first in Western Europe, and something more than a literary interest and respect for certain portions and people in the past. I am inclined to believe that no matter what the next five hundred years may bring, including both recognizable and yet unimaginable changes, appetite and interest in history (in whatever forms) will not diminish—that a consciousness of history, even more than that of the physical sciences, may have been Europe's great lasting contribution to the human mind.

John Lukacs
December 2012

History and the Human Condition

One

History as Literature

History—is it art or science? "History is an art, like the other sciences": a felicitous paradoxical epigram crafted by Veronica Wedgwood, a very erudite and charmingly modest English historian, not inclined to produce epigrams. Here my question is somewhat different. Is the writing of history literary or scientific? Is history literature or science? Well—it *is* literature rather than science. And so it should be. For us.

In the eighteenth century Veronica Wedgwood's epigram would have been a truism, since in that century people did not regard the difference between art and science that is customary to us. We have seen that during that time they saw history as a branch of literature. But we do not and cannot return to the eighteenth century. Our consideration of history is not a return to history as literature but a—somewhat—new recognition.

The emphasis is on letters and words. Let us imagine that at some future time the printed word may cease to exist (except in remnant books or microfilms or other reprintable devices). Will then a film, or any other series of pictures, reconstructing—or, rather, confecting—a then recent or past historical episode amount to authentic history? No, because it will be a necessarily complicated technical construction. History writing (and teaching) are reconstructions too, but their sources are authentic, from men and women who really lived, their acts and words being *retold* but not *reenacted.* And described and told in a common and everyday language, comprehensible to their writers and teachers as well as to their readers. History writing does not depict; it describes.

In the beginning was the word; and then the letter; and then literature. Does history consist of Facts? Yes, there are "facts." The house was burning. The dog did not bark. Julius Caesar crossed the Rubicon. Napoleon lost the war at Waterloo. But "facts" have four limitations at least. One: for us the meaning of every fact exists because of our instant association and comparison of it with other facts. Two: for us the meaning of every fact depends on its statement, on the words with which it is expressed. Three: these words depend on their purposes. There are statements in which the "fact" may be true, but the meaning, the tendency, the purpose of its statement may be false.[1] Fourth: "fact" has its history too. Five or more centuries ago the word *fact* (as also such words as *objective* and *subjective*) meant not what they now mean or are assumed or pretend to mean. Fact meant "feat," something done.

Words are not finite categories but meanings: what they mean to us, for us. They have their own histories and lives and deaths, their powers and their limits. Let us imagine (it is not easy, but imaginable) that at some future time human beings may communicate with each other mostly by pictures, images, numbers, codes. When words will hardly exist, people will not: but their consciousness of history, including their own history, will.

At this late date the recognition that history is literature, rather than science, runs against the determinable inclination to render history more "scientific"—all-encompassing, useful, concrete. The realization (which is not a re-cognition) that the historian must deal with subjects wider and deeper than the records of states and of governments and powers, with more and more people, had led to all kinds of erudite explorations, including social history at its best, but also at its worst. A move in former direction was the French *Annales* school, with superb historians such as Marc Bloch (killed during World War II in 1944) and some of his colleagues and successors producing valuable representations of small as well as large subjects ever since. But now read what the highly reputed French historian Lucien Febvre, once a colleague and then a successor to Bloch, write at the acme of his career, in 1949:

> Like all the sciences history is now evolving rapidly. Certain men are increasingly endeavoring, hesitating and stumbling as they do so, to move in the direction of team work. The day will come when people will talk about "history laboratories" as real things. . . . One or two generations ago the history was an old gentleman sitting in his armchair in front of his index cards which were strictly reserved for his own personal use and as jealously protected against envious rivals as a portfolio in a strongbox; but Anatole

> France's old gentleman and all those described by so many others have come to the end of their curious lives. They have given way to the alert and flexible research director who, having received a very broad education, having been trained to seek in history material with which to look for solutions to the great problems of life which societies and civilizations come up against daily, will be able to map out any investigation, put the right questions, point to precise sources of information, and, having done that, estimate expenditure, control the rotation of equipment, establish the number of staff in each team and launch his workers into a search for the unknown. . . . In a word we shall have to approach things on a far larger scale.[2]

Well—this was (and is) not what happened. During the past sixty years much excellent history has been written and is still being written not by teams but by individual men and women (and by "professionals" as well as "amateurs"), some of them using a computer and yes, many of them their index cards. So much for Lucien Febvre and his "new kind of history"—as, too, for Fernand Braudel and his "total history." Learned historians they, and not devoid of imagination; but, as the French bon mot puts it: *faux bonhommes*, not *quite* good men . . .

However, they are not our problem. That problem is that the broadening of historians' perspectives so often led not to a deepening but to a shallowing of their craft. "Social" (and "gender," "economic," "religious," "intellectual," "sexual") histories are now manifold and rampant. Here is a—*very* random—list of articles and books recently published and reviewed in the *American Historical Review*:

"The Foreign Policy of the Calorie" (Cullather), April 2007

"Clockwatchers and Stargazers: Time Discipline in Early Modern Berlin" (Sautner), June 2007

"The Discomforts of Drag: (Trans) Gender Performance Among Prisoners of War in Russia" (Rachmaninov), April 2006

"Picturing Grief: Soviet Holocaust Photography at the Intersection of History and Memory" (Shneer), 2010

"From 'Black Rice' to 'Brown': Rethinking the History of Risiculture and the Seventeenth and Eighteenth Century Atlantic" (Hawthorne), February 2010

"Thinking Sex in the Transnational Turn" (Canaday), December 2009

"Latin America and the Challenge of Globalizing the History of Sexuality" (Sigal), December 2009

"The Triumph of the Egg" (Freidberg), Annual Article Award, The Berkshire Conference of Women Historians, 2008

"Eye Appeal: The Politics of Sexual Looking in a Consumer Society" (Lindsley), winner of the Aldon Duane Bell Award in Women's History, University of Washington, 2008

"Orgasm in the West: A History of Pleasure from the Sixteenth Century to the Present" (Muchembled), 2009. Reviewed by James R. Farr: "This is a bold book by a great historian."

Alas! These titles need no further comment. Alas! They are not untypical. They prove how low much of the professional historianship, searching for subjects, has sunk.

But what must shock us involves more than the selection of

such subjects. What are the sources for these kinds of topics? What are their evidences? The latter are, practically without exceptions, insufficient and inconsequential. Jacques Barzun said in the 1970s that the current practices of social history are hardly anything more than retrospective sociology. Now let me add that they are, often, not even that. Sociology, with all of its limitations, can be serious and valuable: an exhaustive (and sometimes comprehensive) study of a society or of a definite portion of it. But the above-listed examples are not that. They are attempts at a scientific sociography (which is almost a contradiction in itself). The aims of sociology is definition. The aim of sociography is description—whence it is, inevitably, literary and historical.

Literary, rather than "scientific." There is a concordance here (at least partial) between history and the novel. Just about every novel is sociographical; it tells us the things about people and their society in a certain place at a certain time. Not every history is sociographical: not every historical subject does necessarily include the description of a society of a certain time. But *description* is what they have in common. ("Description," even more than mere "narrative.") A choice of words, phrases, sentences, nouns as well as adjectives or adverbs, of significances and sequences, of meanings: choices that are more than stylistic—they are moral. There may be a moral purpose behind a scientific statement, but there is nothing that is moral or immoral in its mathematic accuracy. But the purpose of history is understanding even more than accuracy (though not without a creditable respect for the latter).

And this is at least one reason why historians ought to read literature, and even more than statistics: to truly widen and deepen their acquaintance with their chosen subject, but also to recognize that their main task is a kind of literature, rather than a kind of science. The converse of this desideratum has been stated recently by the Polish poet Adam Zagajewski:

> I am not a historian, but I'd like literature to assume, consciously and in all seriousness, the function of a historical chronicle. I don't want it to follow the example set by modern historians, cold fish by and large, who spend their lives in vanquished archives and write in an inhuman, ugly, wooden, bureaucratic language from which all poetry's been driven, a language flat as a wood louse and petty as the daily paper. I'd like it to return to earlier examples, maybe even Greek, to the ideal of the historian-poet, a person who either has seen and experienced what he describes for himself, or has drawn upon a living oral tradition, his family's or his tribe's, who doesn't fear engagement and emotion, but who cares nonetheless about his story's truthfulness.

"His story's truthfulness." Ah! there the dog lies buried. (And there too the dangers lie.)

Yes, the state of academic history writing is bad, though not quite how this good Polish poet states it. There are still many historians (with their index cards). Zagajewski's exhortation is: "Literature! Writers! Get into, get with history!" My exhortation is the reverse: Historians! Get into, get with literature!

Well-written history is still being produced (and will be produced) by professional historians. More well-written history is, and will be, produced by "amateur"—that is, nonprofessional—historians. Because of this I must sum up something about the relationship of "professionals" and "amateurs" writing history.

Some things ought to be obvious. The distinction between professionals and amateurs writing history may exist, but it makes less sense than it does in other disciplines. A professional brain surgeon should perform a brain operation, an amateur not. But to say that a poet must have a PhD in poetry is an absurdity. To say that a historian must have a PhD in history is not an absurdity, but somehow in between the case of the brain surgeon and that of the poet. The other, related but also obvious, matter is that "amateur," that is, nonprofessional, nonacademic, noncertified historians have often produced excellent, on occasion magisterial books, better than those written by professionals about the same or related subjects. So we may go as far as to state that when it comes to history writing (and also to historical research), a distinction between professionals and nonprofessionals may exist, but it is not a categorical difference.

After all, the instrument of their craft is the same: everyday language. We have seen that in England the literary tradition lasted longer, and the consideration of history as a science came somewhat reluctantly later than in most other countries. But during the twentieth century the relationship between academic and nonacademic historians became more complicated, even in England. Professional historians have been (and often are) jealous of the public success of their amateur confrères, while nonprofessionals, on occasion, reveal a sometimes uneasy respect for established professionals.[3] Yet in some countries, Austria, for example histories about the first half of the twentieth century, and especially about Hitler, are by such master historians as Friedrich Heer and Brigitte Hamann, who have no academic appointment. (Hitler remains a particular case. Of the almost one thousand books and biographies written about him, the best are not by professional historians,[4] including even the excellent and conscientious Ian Kershaw.)

There are reasons for this. One is that the "amateur" historians are often more literary than their academic competitors. (In so many instances their love for literature led them to history, whereas for many academics their interest in history may lead them to consider, here and there, literature—but not necessarily so: their main interest may still be the reading of the works of other professionals.) Another reason (or, rather, condition) is that some amateurs may know more of the world—including human types—than do professionals, ever so often confining their lives within their academic circles. Here is an example that, in a moment, struck me like a splendid spark. In the second volume of his magisterial work about the Franco-Russian alliance of 1894 (*The Fateful Alliance: France, Russia, and the Coming of the First World War*, 1984), George Kennan described the chief of the French Army Staff, General Boisdeffre, better than Boisdeffre's portrait limned by no lesser novelist than Marcel Proust in *Jean Santeuil*. The latter was not at all a book about the Franco-Russian alliance; but Kennan read it.[5]

Historians: please hear what Jacob Burckhardt told his (few) students in Basel, that history has really no method, but you must know how to read. (*What*, *how*, and *when*.) Three hundred years ago Lady Mary Wortley Montagu: "No entertainment is as cheap as reading, nor any pleasure so lasting." (The first past of this sentence is no longer so [television, movies]—the second, yes.)[6]

In 1932 Christopher Dawson replied to Alan Bullock (in "The Problem of Metahistory"), "The academic historian is perfectly right in insisting on the techniques of historical criticism and research. But the mastery of these techniques will not produce great history, any more than a mastery of metrical technique will produce great poetry." "Bisogna saper leggere": poetry, anecdotes, jokes, all kinds of stories may help to understand a past.[7]

So historians must read and know what to read—a knowledge and an interest and, yes, an appetite that will not only enrich their minds but guide and inspire their writing. In the long sad history of mankind, we know of a few genius poets and writers who read little. But good historians? No. Yet I know many historians who have deprived their minds *and* their research of their topics by ignoring the literature of that period. An acquaintance of mine whose main professional interest was British liberal politics in the 1960s consistently refused to read Trollope. Another acquaintance whose "field" was the Enlightenment did not read Tocqueville's *Old Regime and the French Revolution*.

Tocqueville is a good case in point. Those who occasionally recognized what he in the *Ancien Régime* attempted (successfully), who saw that in his going beneath the colorful surface of events he was doing something profound and new, were French literary critics, not historians. There has been evolution here, but even now Tocqueville is classified as a social and political thinker rather than a historian. Or consider his brilliant memoir of the 1848 revolutions (originally written only for himself and then discovered by a nephew forty years later in a desk). These *Recollections* of 1848 are exceptional in their perspicacity and style.

What happened, and what people then thought and perhaps still think happened, may be found in a variety of sources, in some places (and times) hidden, in others not. To search for them is, or should be, the unavoidable duty of serious professional historians. And even those among them who respect literature must understand that the quality (and even the style) of writing is more than a matter of literary technique. A historian (and a good one) once said to me that, yes, historians often refrain from employing adjectives that could enliven their narrative accounts. True—even though the mark of good writing resides less in adjectives than in verbs. (James Joyce in *Dubliners*: "She sat at the window, watching the evening invade the avenue.")

For an honest historian his duty includes, involves, both writing and teaching—even when he is not speaking in a classroom. He also ought to know that the relationship between the spoken and the written word is not simple. Speech, contrary to Freud's doctrine (and perhaps also to Joyce's idea in *Ulysses*), is more than an outcome of thought: it is the realization of it. When it comes to writing, I cannot but agree with T. S. Eliot—that the motive to write is the desire to vanquish a mental preoccupation by expressing it consciously and clearly. But in speaking as well as in writing, the choice of every word is not only an aesthetic or a technical but a moral choice. Of this historians ought to be even more aware than are other writers in other professions.

There is much that historians have yet to learn. Especially now when the chaotic crisis in all kinds of disciplines—indeed, of civilization itself—has reached the historical profession. They have to confront the conditions of their knowledge—indeed, of all human knowledge—for the sake of the health and the future of their discipline. For now, at the end of the age, when the concept and the ideal of Objectivity have faded, there are new dangers already apparent. One of them is Subjectivity (involved with "postmodernism").

If knowledge of the past (again, like all kinds of human knowledge) is *participant*, is that designation not necessarily *subjective*? It is not, because Subjectivism, as also Objectivism, tends to be (and actually is) determinist. I have previously suggested that the cultural and civilizational crisis seems to have reached the historical profession around 1960, a necessarily inaccurate dating. But it may be significant that 1961 was the publication date of *What Is History?* by Edward Hallett Carr (his Trevelyan Lectures), a book that, we are told, has sold hundreds of thousands of copies since then. Forty years later there was a symposium commemorating Carr's book, held at the Institute of Historical Research in London. *What Is History?* is "the classic we celebrate and commemorate," said and wrote one of the speakers (Professor Linda Colley). Another contributor (Professor Alice Kessler-Harris): "My generation of graduate students in the U.S. cut their teeth on E. H. Carr." (Much orthodontic treatment still needed.) And what did Carr pronounce? "Before you study the history, study the historian." According to Carr, the historian's background—especially his social background—virtually determines the history he writes. Well, how about some of the sons (and daughters) of rich bourgeois who became Marxists, or the offspring of Jewish Marxists who chose to become conservatives? In any event, by 1961 the once rigidly economic (and pro-Soviet) determinist Carr moved, or slid, into another version of determinism, a subjectivist one.[8] (Consider that subjective determinism was also the essence of Adolf Hitler's convictions about human nature: "Jews can only think in a Jewish way." His idealist determinism: "We will win because our ideas are stronger and better than those of our opponents." Otherwise history makes no sense.)

And—an important "and" for us—still Carr kept on insisting that history was, and is, a Science. He could not free himself from the Objective-Subjective terminology. In *What Is History?* he wrote: "It does not follow that, because a mountain appears to take on different angles of vision, it has *objectively* [my italics] no shape at all, or an infinity of shapes." But the more "objective" our concept of the shape of the mountain, the more abstract that mountain becomes. Even more important historically: the existence of the mountain was meaningless until men appeared, and then saw it, and eventually called it "a mountain," different from other protuberances. Much, much later did someone conceive it as an "objective fact."

In sum, perspective is a component of reality. Participation is the—inevitable—inseparability of the knower from the known. There is now a corresponding recognition of this condition in physics, too: that the "subject" of the search or re-search of subatomic matter is not matter "itself" but the physicist's investigation of matter. Many physicists are unwilling to think about this, just as many historians are unwilling to think about the limitations of their "objectivity." Is the latter an acknowledgment of human limitations? Yes, it is: yet it is the kind of acknowledgment that does not reduce but enriches the functioning and the qualities of our minds.[9]

The future of history lies there. The knower and the known are not identical, but they are inseparable. That is, too, how we, on this earth, are at the center of the universe. We did not create the universe; but we invented it, time after time.

Our knowledge of history is of course less than the entire past, but it is also more than the recorded past. But the remembered past is also incomplete, and fallible, and ever changing. Memory brings something from a past into a present; it is a function not unique to human beings. But while we are not only responsible for what we think, we are responsible, too, for what we remember—or, more precisely, what we choose to remember. (And memory has its history, too—a famous passage from Dante: "Nothing is more miserable than remembering good times in times of woe." Many of us, in the twentieth century, remember that such memories could be sustaining.)

The historian's choice of his subject is governed by his interests. But what kinds of interests? Looking at some of the recent subjects chosen by professional historians, recognizing the absurdity of some of them, already involves a question: What was the essence of their interest? How did they become interested in their subject? Were they really inspired by their choice? "How" and "really"—was their interest more or less authentic? Or was their choice the outcome of a personal concern involving their professional careers? The unavoidable relationship of the knower with the known does not mean that the knower and the known are identical—nor is the character of a historian and the worth of his subject.

When, say, three hundred years ago an early frost destroyed a peasant's crops, this change in his material conditions during a then cruel winter meant very much. But what was he thinking? We (unlike God) may know little or nothing about that. In any event, did his thinking affect the material state of his existence? Perhaps not much. In our mass democratic age conditions are different. The value of everything, material as well as intellectual and spiritual, is what people think it is. That has always been so, at least to some extent; but less than it has become. (This is what I have dared to call a mental intrusion into the structure of events—we may even go so far as to call it an increasing spiritualization [and abstraction] of matter.) This of course runs against the accepted belief that we now live in an overwhelmingly materialistic world, and that people are overwhelmingly materialistic. Yet what people—whether individual persons or masses of people—think *is* the fundamental essence of what happens in this world, the material products and institutions of it being the consequences, indeed the superstructures. And what people think and believe—and what people thought and believed—are matters (yes: matters) that, with their documented evidences notwithstanding, are difficult to trace. (And, in re-searching such matters, literature may be a better guide than science.)

This is not a proposition of categorical idealism. Ideas and beliefs are not abstractions, they are historical, like everything human. But they are not the obvious outcomes of some kind of *Zeitgeist*. Repeat: recognize that people do not *have* ideas. They choose them. (And how, or why, and when they choose?—difficult questions these.) Here is my disagreement with the neo-idealist R. G. Collingwood, who—a subjectivist determinist—recognizing that a German historian who was born in 1900 would see the past differently from a French historian who was born in 1800, concludes: "There is no point in asking which was the right point of view. Each was the only one possible for the man who adopted it." *The only one possible?* That French historian born in 1800 could have been a monarchist, or a republican, or a Bonapartist; a Germanophile or a Germanophobe—that German historian born in 1900 could prefer to read and write about Louis XIV, or that French historian born in 1800 about Friedrich Wilhelm I. There is the perennial condition that people will tend to adjust their ideas to circumstances (or what they think those circumstances are), rather than adjust circumstances to their ideas. One

large consequence of this is the slow change of movements of political beliefs. Again—entirely contrary to Marx et al.—these movements are seldom the results of material conditions. What marks the movements in the history of societies and peoples is not the accumulation of capital. It is the accumulation of opinions. (And such accumulations can be promoted, and for some time even produced, by manipulations of publicity, confected for the majority by hard small minorities—though not always, and not forever.)

Beyond and beneath the difficult task of reconstructing what people thought, and of the growing influence of mind into matter, is the phenomenon of inflation, another fundamentally democratic development. When there is more and more of something, it tends to be worth less and less. Consider, if only for a moment, the now virtual disappearance of the once inflation-deflation "business cycles." What we now have is a constant inflation, though at varying speeds. And the inflation of words and slogans, of categories and standards, of pictures and images, led to the inflation of money and of possessions, especially in nations where creditability (a potential) has become more important than actual possession (that may be legally "owned" but is, in reality, rented). This, often dangerous and also artificial, spiritualization of matter has led to more and more abstractions influencing people. (And here again, consider once more the benefices of literature—which, when good, abhors an inflation of words.)

But this intrusion of minds into the structure of events renders description more and more difficult, because no matter how much information is available about them, "simple" people are no longer very simple. And, of course, neither are educated ones. When reading Dickens or Balzac, Thackeray or Flaubert, Trollope or Conrad or *Buddenbrooks*, we learn easily not only *what* but *how* Gradgrind or Goriot's daughters or Becky Sharp or Charles Bovary or Dr. Grantly or Kurtz or Tony Buddenbrook, whether major or minor characters, were thinking, how they used their minds. About a man or woman living in New York in 2011—what is, what may be, going on in their minds? No simple attribution will do. Or was Dwight D. Eisenhower a simpler man than was Ulysses S. Grant? He was not.

And so a thoughtful historian must direct his attention not only to *what* ideas have been current but to *how* and *why* they had arisen and then invaded and even changed the histories of peoples. And to this he must add the very historical question: *when?* Again it was Kierkegaard who uttered a profound and yet commonsensical truth: "It is possible to be *both* good and bad, but it is impossible *at one and the same time* to become both good and bad." (This amounts to more than even another truthful maxim about human nature crafted by La Rochefoucauld: "There are evil men who would be less dangerous were it not that they have something good in them too.") Kierkegaard's statement is about God's creation of *time.* It is also an answer to the uneasy question of some people about someone like Hitler. In *The Hitler of History*, I wrote: "Yes, there was plenty of evil in Hitler's expressed thoughts, wishes, statements, and decisions. (I emphasize *expressed*, since that is what evidence allows us to consider.) But keep in mind that evil as well as good is part of human nature. Our inclinations to evil (whether they mature into acts or not) are reprehensible but also normal. To deny that human condition leads us to the assertion that Hitler was abnormal; and the simplistic affixing of the 'abnormal' label to Hitler relieves him, again, of responsibility—indeed, categorically so."[10] The Hitler who was kind to children and to his dog and the Hitler who wished and

ordered the elimination of entire peoples was the same person, at different times.

When? All prose literature is concerned with *when?* Earlier I wrote that a fact is inseparable from its statement, and that its statement is hardly separable from its purpose, and that the purpose of historians should now be the reduction of untruths. In 1994 I also wrote: "I must now add something to this: [There is] the inevitable historicity—which does not mean relativity—of human truth. To say 'A black man is as good as any of you' at a Ku Klux Klan Konclave in 1915 is something different from saying the same words to a liberal audience in 1970. To say (and not merely mutter): "A German Jew is worth more than a Viennese Nazi" in a crowded Munich streetcar in 1942 is something very different from pronouncing the same words at an anti-Nazi rally in New York in 1942 (or to a Berlin audience in, say, 1972). This is obvious. But I am not speaking merely of different kinds of courage. I am attempting to suggest that the statement at the Ku Klux Klan rally in 1915 or the statement in the Munich streetcar in 1942 may not have been entire truths, but somehow *truer* than the same statements at another time and in another place. Because they were exceptional. And in history—more than in science—exceptions do matter.

Every good novelist knows this. So should every good historian.

Two

American "Exceptionalism"

In the *Oxford English Dictionary* the word *exceptionalism* does not exist. It became current lately among American historians—reason enough to form the substance of Professor Alonzo Hamby's thoughtful essay in the May/June 2008 *Historically Speaking*. Still, allow me to ask: Does exceptionalism differ much from patriotism, or from nationalism, or from populism? We may distinguish certain nuances: the sense of his country's uniqueness by a traditionalist patriot differs from the aggressive exceptionalism of a populist nationalist. And, beyond semantic distinctions, ought we not recognize that many nations other than the United States, thinking about their culture and history, consider themselves exceptional? Yet American inclination to think that the history and the destiny of the United States are exceptional has been powerful and widespread enough to amount to a belief that Americans are "a chosen people" (an inclination that had led to the perils of other peoples in the past).

Hamby is right to suggest that the societies and the living standards of the United States and of other peoples, especially in Western Europe, have now become more alike. But what are involved here are more than social and material developments. Hence my addenda.

In the nineteenth century America and Europe moved in opposite directions. The United States expanded westward; the European powers eastward and southward. The great events in the history of the United States were the westward movement, the Civil War, and mass immigration. The great events in the history of Europe were three series of revolutions, and after them short wars between great states, leading to the unification of Germany (and of Italy). But in the twentieth century (more precisely, in the historical and somewhat short twentieth century, from 1914 to 1989), the two greatest events, the two enormous mountain ranges, both for Europe and America were the same. They were the two world wars (of the last of which the so-called Cold War was but a consequence).

There was another difference between America and Europe in the nineteenth century, and then another convergence in the twentieth century. In the nineteenth century the great political divisions in America and Europe were different. In Europe, and in England, the division and the debate were mostly between conservatives and liberals. In the United States there was no conservative party. But sometime around 1870 in Europe and Britain, this conservative vs. liberal dichotomy or difference began to weaken. And what followed was not their Hegelian synthesis: instead, two new great movements grew. One was nationalism; the other was socialism. And while in the nineteenth century the political categories and their terminology in Europe and England were not applicable to the United States, in the twentieth century, by and large, they were and are still now: of our two great political parties the Republicans being more nationalist than socialist, the Democrats more socialist than nationalist. Argue this, if you so wish, but then consider, too, how at the same time the designations of "conservative" and "liberal" have been losing much of their meaning;[1] and so has not only Frederick Jackson Turner's frontier theory but the theses of some of its historian critics, too.

Hamby is also right to suggest that most eminent American historians around 1950, while dubious about the frontier thesis, still took American exceptionalism for granted. Yet I wish to add what, in retrospect, reveals an amazing shortsightedness of these celebrated historians. Look at the dates of their works (still often regarded as "seminal"), as cited by Hamby: Potter (1954), Boorstin (1953), Hartz (1955), Hofstadter (1948), to which let me add Lionel Trilling (*The Liberal Imagination*, 1950, not mentioned by Hamby). One thesis there is in all of them: unlike in Europe or elsewhere in the world, there is only one intellectual tradition in the United States, a perennially liberal one. Now consider: these men wrote their books, their general theses, sweeping across the American mental and political and ideological landscape *at the very time*, 1950–55, when in the United States a popular movement started to appear and rise that, for the first time, chose to call itself "conservative." And less than thirty years later, more Americans chose to designate themselves as conservatives than as liberals; indeed the latter had become an unseemly adjective, a bad word to be shunned. Since I have written about this elsewhere, I am restating some of the stunning landmarks of this political landslide in an endnote.[2]

And, besides the above-mentioned shortsightedness of the then leading American historians, one last remark, the essence of which is more than merely terminological: ever since 1950 the American "conservative" movement, its adherents, and the majority of Republican voters have been busy nationalists rather than true conservatives. They are the true believers in American exceptionalism, frontier thesis or not. Here I arrive at the principal addendum to Hamby's essay. For a wise and profound dismissal of both the frontier thesis and American exceptionalism was pronounced by Professor Carlton J. H. Hayes in 1945, and read as his presidential address of the American Historical Association (AHA) that December. The very circumstances of this event deserve some attention.

Hayes was the most eminent American historian of modern Europe. His *Political and Cultural History of Modern Europe*, first published in 1916, with several amended editions, remained the classic two-volume history of that great subject for at least thirty years: a singular achievement. There are two significant matters about Hayes's election in 1945. One, involving the election, is academic and ephemeral. The other, involving his presidential address, is much more than that.

In 1942 President Roosevelt asked Hayes to accept the post of ambassador to Franco's Spain. That may have been the best of Roosevelt's often odd ambassadorial appointments. Hayes's wartime mission to Spain (which would be the title of his subsequent recollection of it) was quite successful. He was instrumental in the gradual, though uneasy, movement of Franco's regime from its political and ideological alliance with Hitler's Germany to something like a cautious neutrality. More than sixty years later there is a general consensus among historians, Americans, British, German, and Spanish, about Hayes's merits. But this was not so in 1945. Liberal publications had criticized Hayes, stating—wrongly—that this Catholic scholar was an appeaser of Generalissimo Franco. A result of this was the unusual—indeed, unique—challenge of his election for president of the AHA. Several influential American historians, among them Richard Hofstadter, Kenneth Stampp, and Frank Friedel, opposed Hayes's election. All kinds of faculty-club intrigues and letter writings followed, whereafter Hayes was elected by a vote of 110 to 66. That ephemeral storm in the academic teacup suggests the ideological myopia of some of its participants, an event that many of them preferred to forget thereafter. It may deserve a footnote in an intellectual history of America during the Second World War, though not more.

But what is important for our purposes is the text of Hayes's presidential address, printed, as customary, in the next (January 1946) number of the *American Historical Review*. Its title was: "The American Frontier—Frontier of What?" It was a trenchant criticism of Turner's famous thesis, especially of its influence on American history since that time:

> [The time has come] when our historians might profitably broaden their conception of the frontier. . . . It is a frontier of what? . . . [The] advancing frontier of North America, like similar frontiers in South America, Australasia . . . is a frontier of Europe. . . . [People and historians] assumed that the frontier was a peculiarly American phenomenon, determining the unique character of our own national society and culture. [T]his restricted interpretation . . . and the concurrent neglect of broader and otherwise obvious considerations have been, I submit, at once a result and a stimulant of growing intellectual isolationism . . . a lurking suspicion of inferiority, which long lingered with us, has had the usual psychological compensation in strident

> assertions of superiority. . . . [This] trend, if unchecked, can only confirm the popular myths that the "American way of life" is something entirely indigenous, something wholly new, and something vastly superior to any other nation's. It is also likely to strengthen our people's missionary and messianic impulse, which will have far greater scope and far greater opportunity for expressing itself in the current aftermath of the Second World War, and which . . . may lead to the most dangerous consequences for the United States itself. . . .
>
> "European," as I here use the term, does not refer merely to a detached piece of geography . . . or a hoary and pitiable Old World. Rather it refers to a great historic culture, the "Western" civilization, which, taking its rise around the Mediterranean, has long since embraced the Atlantic. . . . Of such an Atlantic community and the European civilization basic to it, we Americans are co-heirs and co-developers, and probably in the future the leaders. . . . [We must discern and take] our rightful place in an international regional community of which Atlantic is the inland sea.

There was (and remains) something prophetic in this magisterial essay. During the first one hundred years in the history of the United States, the main American ethos was that of a definite distance and difference between the New and the Old World. But in 1898 and thereafter the United States became a world power. There followed its intervention in two world wars, helping to rescue Western Europe. A reverse movement: for about three hundred years, millions of people from Europe crossed the Atlantic westward, and so moved the American "frontier" and empire westward. But in 1917–18, for the first time, more than one million Americans were sent across the Atlantic eastward, to help decide a great European war. In the Second World War this would happen again, to a greater extent. However, who thought then that this American military presence in Europe would be permanent? President Roosevelt was an internationalist; he put much effort and hope into creating a new institution, the United Nations. But he, too, believed that after the war millions of American soldiers in Europe must come home, and soon. He was much aware of what was still there of American "isolationist" sentiment.

That was not what happened. Less than four years after Hayes's presidential address, a permanent American military presence was firmly established in western and southern Europe (and soon even Spain would become part of it). The North Atlantic Treaty Organization came into being because of what seemed then the preponderant Russian and communist power in Eastern Europe. There developed a conflation of American and Western European interests and connections, on more than one level. The American "frontier" was now in the middle of Europe, along the so-called iron curtain. The Truman and Marshall and Acheson policy, crystallizing in 1948–49, seemed the final victory of American internationalism over that of American isolationism. (The latter was always anti-European rather than anti-Asian, suspicious of American involvements in Europe, suspicious of European influences in America.)[3] But that, too, did not last. American isolationism was, of course, American exceptionalism *pur et simple*. But was it really *pur et simple?* Soon after 1950 most of the isolationists of 1940 became advocates of a worldwide crusade against the Soviet Union. In 1956 Section Nine of the Republican Party platform called "for the establishment of American air and naval bases all around the world." (This was the party still called "isolationist" by some journalists and liberals, even at that time.)

Do Americans know more about Europe—and about the world!—than they did fifty years ago? Proponents of "multiculturalism" direct American interests not to Europe but to other "world cultures"; the once required basic courses in "Western civilization" have, by and large, disappeared from American universities, colleges, and high schools. In his address in 1945 Carlton Hayes castigated "the fads" of "curriculum-makers": "I, for one, do not see how we substantially improve matters by expanding a high school course in American history from one year to two or three years and telescoping all the rest . . . into a single year or half year of fleeting elementary generalizations quaintly described as 'world history.'"[4] As true today as in 1945.

But, sixty years later, where is the American frontier? Or, to put it more accurately, is there any American frontier left? Even more important, does American exceptionalism justify the advocates (many of them former liberals) of American hegemony over the world? They may not be willing to listen to John Quincy Adams's warning in 1821 that, while we are friends of liberty in the world, we "do not go abroad in search of monsters to destroy." But they ought to listen to what the lonely young George Kennan wrote in 1940, forlorn in the capital of the then triumphant Third Reich: "No people is great enough to establish world hegemony." As true today as it was in 1940—and something that even our most benevolent exceptionalists should keep in their minds.

Three

The Germans' Two Wars: Heisenberg and Bohr

I begin with something that is (or should be) obvious. The history of the atomic bomb (more accurately: the history of the first three atomic bombs, Alamogordo, Hiroshima, Nagasaki) is part of the history of the Second World War. The history of these bombs—as indeed the history of every human product—is the history of the men and women who invented them, designed them, planned them, and constructed them. The history of science not only is inseparable from the history of scientists: it *is* the history of scientists. No scientists, no science. This is because history is not part of science, while "science" is part of the history of mankind.

The "causes" of the atom bomb are historical and, ultimately, personal; they are scientific and technical only on a secondary and mechanical level of "causes." The causes of the making of the bomb during the Second World War were Hitler and also the persecution of Jews by his Germans. The first atomic bomb was made when it was made not merely because at a certain phase in the development of applied physics a certain stage of technical capacity was reached, but because at a certain time in history the fear had arisen in the minds of a few eminent scientists, most of them refugees in America, that German scientists might be building an atomic bomb for Hitler. Technically speaking, the important stages in the history of the atomic bomb were the splitting of a uranium nucleus by neutrons in Berlin in December 1938, the functioning of the first nuclear reactor in Chicago in December 1942, the exploding of the first bomb in New Mexico in July 1945, and the two bombs finally cast on Japan in August 1945. But the technical achievement of these stages must not obscure their main purposes, which, as in every historical event, were the results of personal choices, their sources having been the national, political, religious, intellectual, and ideological inclinations in the minds of responsible men.

At the very beginning of the war, more than two years before Pearl Harbor, the ruling powers of the United States were told that an atomic bomb could be made, and that it *must* be made, because Germany might be making it. The ruling powers of National Socialist Germany were told somewhat later that atomic bombs could be made but that the costs and the efforts and the duration of their production were unduly large. In both countries the construction of a nuclear reactor was necessary before the production of a nuclear bomb, but German scientists, though having come close, had not reached that stage before the end of the war and the total defeat of Germany. But my subject here is not the actual race between American and German bomb building—nor within that, the awful and unanswerable question of potentiality, of what could have happened had Hitler possessed atomic bombs.

My subject includes a meeting between two scientists, the German Werner Heisenberg and the Danish Niels Bohr, in German-occupied Copenhagen in September 1941, about which many books and many dozens of articles and a very successful play have been written and international conferences assembled, more than sixty years after that event. Heisenberg and Bohr talked and listened to and understood and misunderstood each other. What Heisenberg said (or suggested) was (and remained) more significant than how Bohr responded to him. That imbalance (if that was what it was) was well-nigh inevitable because of the very circumstances and conditions of their meeting and also what had preceded their conversations in September 1941.

Heisenberg and Bohr were among the greatest—and, perhaps, *the* greatest—physicists in the twentieth century. Surely they were the two leaders during the brief golden age of physics, 1924–27, when Heisenberg's indeterminacy theory and Bohr's Copenhagen complementary interpretation superseded Einstein's still largely deterministic concept of physical reality. Heisenberg and Bohr were close allies at the time, leaving aside Einstein (who was unable and unwilling to accept the meaning of indeterminacy even against its evidences, and who tried in vain to disprove it during the last thirty years of his life). Heisenberg, fifteen years younger than Bohr, was his protégé. Soon Heisenberg's reputation rose even higher. They regarded each other with mutual high esteem; but they were also close friends, talking about everything, spending skiing and mountain vacations together, enjoying music (Heisenberg was a good pianist). Heisenberg went often to see Bohr in Copenhagen. Almost always they talked in German, but Heisenberg even learned to speak Danish more or less adequately. Heisenberg was German, Bohr was Danish and half-Jewish. This did not matter—surely not for some time.

In 1933 Hitler came to power in Germany. In the same year Heisenberg, at the age of thirty-two, won the Nobel Prize in Physics. Like many patriotic Germans he saw something good in the end of the tottering Weimar Republic and in the national rejuvenation of which Hitler was the loudest drummer and most strident trumpeter. Heisenberg never became a National Socialist Party member. He regarded the excesses of Nazi rhetoric and behavior as regrettable—and, more important, as perhaps temporary: he thought and often said that things and people would settle down sooner or later, and then normal conditions of work and life could prevail. He helped to protect and to assist some Jewish physicists who were deprived of their jobs and felt compelled to leave Germany in 1933 and after. There were instances when he tried to persuade some of them not to leave or even to return (he so advised Max Born, a colleague whom he admired, in a letter, including a suggestion that not everything was bad—indeed, that there were some splendid things happening—in the new Germany). He refused to agree with two older German Nobel Prize–winning physicists, Philipp Lenard and Johannes Stark, who were furiously anti-Jewish, bellowing together against Einstein and his theories and "Jewish physics." Consequently in 1937 articles in a newspaper of the *SS* attacked Heisenberg (who was newly married then), calling him "a white Jew" on one occasion. Eventually, possibly because of the intervention of Heinrich Himmler (Heisenberg's mother knew Himmler's mother), Heisenberg was exonerated. His life and work could go on undisturbed; that same year he and Bohr met again, at an international physicists' conference.

In late 1938 something unexpected occurred in a physics laboratory in Berlin, the meaning of which was immediately recognized by top physicists throughout the world. Otto Hahn (a decent and anti-Nazi German who was to receive the Nobel Prize in Chemistry in 1945, while he was still interned in England) and Fritz Strassmann (an exceptionally principled Austrian whose bravery in helping and hiding Jews during the war would eventually be honored by the state of Israel) found, after repeated experiments, that uranium atoms could be split when bombarded by neutrons, that such a "fission" resulted in unexpected and powerful by-products. Hahn had visited Bohr in Copenhagen in October, speaking about his experiments in a lecture; Bohr was skeptical but encouraged Hahn to go on with his experiments. A few weeks later, in December, Hahn's experiments concluded that fission could be achieved, that the split mass could be converted to energy. Heisenberg, teaching and working in Leipzig, learned of the Hahn achievement in Berlin from Carl Friedrich von Weizsaecker, who was, in a way, Heisenberg's protégé before that time.[1] Soon—in early 1939—Hahn published the results of his experiments in a German scientific journal; a similar account would follow in a British one.

Less than a month after Hahn's conclusive experiment, Bohr sailed for the United States, where he would spend part of a semester at Princeton. He understood the importance of the fission, but he thought that a consequent chain reaction could not lead to the making of a bomb, since the extent of such a construction would have to be so large as to be practically impossible. He said this in public and kept to this belief for some time.[2] He sailed back to Copenhagen in April 1939, only a few weeks before Heisenberg arrived for an American lecture tour. He was invited to some of the same universities that Bohr had visited; and, more significantly, by many of the top physicists of the world now gathered in the United States, most of them refugees from Hitler's Germany and Mussolini's Italy. There is no evidence that Heisenberg behaved and talked with much compunction or caution or even excessive reserve with his colleagues, many of them Jewish, meeting them in their universities and sometimes in their homes. There are many records and memories of their conversations. They attempted to persuade him—so did eminent native-born American physicists—to remain in the United States, where he could work amid the best of conditions for his research, especially since the war in Europe was coming nearer and nearer. He would not give that a thought. His family and wife and first child were of course in Germany, awaiting his return. More important—certainly in the minds of his former colleagues and friends—was their concern with what Hitler's Germany represented and where the war could lead. One telling evidence of Heisenberg's convictions (and of his inclinations) is how he answered the great Italian physicist Fermi, an old friend (whose wife was Jewish). Talking with Fermi, he said that he felt a duty not to separate himself from young German scientists who, unlike himself, could not travel easily out of Germany. Fermi then got to the gist of the matter. The current German regime could force German physicists to work toward the potential manufacture of atomic weapons. Heisenberg said that he understood Fermi but that it was his opinion that such a technical achievement would in any event last longer than the war. In one, only one, instance Heisenberg spoke with something like anger. Fermi's wife said that anyone remaining in Germany must be mad; Heisenberg was hurt, and refuted her vehemently. He left New York in August 1939, sailing home on a half-empty German liner.

Heisenberg and Einstein had not met that summer in the United States. But exactly one month before the outbreak of the war, Albert Einstein signed a letter addressed directly to Franklin Roosevelt, advising him of the danger that the discovery of fission might enable Germany to construct a hitherto unimaginably powerful weapon, suggesting that the American government's support was needed for an American achievement of such a bomb. The idea of such a letter arose in the minds of the Hungarian-born physicists Leo Szilard and Eugene Wigner as early as June. Knowing of Einstein's reputation, Szilard and Wigner drove out to his summer dwelling to make him write to Roosevelt. Einstein wrote the letter and sent it to an acquaintance, a Jewish financier who had access to the president.[3] Let me repeat: my concern in this chapter is not the race between the American and the German bomb making. It is Heisenberg and Bohr: more precisely, how they regarded each other and how others saw them; even more precisely, how and why Heisenberg came to Bohr during the war, and how Bohr then came to regard Heisenberg's character and his politics. The sequence of events in 1939 suggests that many, if not most, of the refugee physicists, beyond and beneath their regret that they were not able to persuade Heisenberg to leave Germany for good, had begun to worry that Heisenberg would (or might) work for the achievement of nuclear explosives in Hitler's Third Reich. In sum: they trusted (and often admired) Heisenberg's science; they did not admire (and often did not trust) his politics. That, in essence, cast a shadow—at least in their minds—on his character.

"What kind of a man is Heisenberg?" the refugee scientists

and their American colleagues asked themselves and one another. In a chapter on "The Question of Scientific Certitude"[4] a few years ago, I wrote: "After all, everything that a man does depends on some kind of belief. He will speak and act in a certain way *because* he thinks that this kind of speaking or acting is better than another. 'What kind of a man' is not a simple question of category but one that inevitably depends on the inclinations of his mind and on the ideas he prefers to choose." And Heisenberg was, evidently, a German patriot, perhaps even a nationalist: his first duty was perhaps to but certainly *in* Germany. That his former colleagues knew, and their own conclusions sprang therefrom.

On September 1, 1939, German armies invaded Poland and the Second World War began. Fourteen days later Heisenberg wrote a letter to Bohr, carried to Denmark by a mutual acquaintance, a Japanese physicist. "So once more I have the chance to write you. You know how sad I am about this entire development. But all of us have seen it coming, in America. I came back, since I belong here. You will surely understand this?"[5] Bohr did not know that some of his American colleagues had begun to promote the prospect of constructing an atomic bomb; nor that the Heereswaffenamt (rough translation: Office of Military Weaponry) in Berlin had convened German physicists to discuss the problems and the prospect of manufacturing atomic explosives. He did not think that this was yet technically feasible (he said this in a lecture in Copenhagen later in 1939).

On April 9, 1940, Hitler ordered the German army and navy to occupy Denmark and Norway. Suddenly that brought about an additional drama in the lives of the two physicists. Only a day before the German invasion, Bohr had been in Oslo, at a scientific conference attended by the king of Norway himself; his ferry brought him back to Copenhagen on the very morning of the German invasion. The refugee scientist Lise Meitner, who had moved from Germany through Holland to Sweden in 1938, found herself in Copenhagen on April 9, and then quickly fled back to her safe harbor in Sweden on the same day, taking with her among other things a letter from Bohr.

There is no evidence of any correspondence between Heisenberg and Bohr after April 1940. Surely Heisenberg was concerned with the fate of his former patron and friend, but it seems that he thought it best not to contact him until early September 1941.[6] That he respected Bohr was known by many people, including some within the government of the Third Reich; it may have contributed to the condition that Bohr's work in his Physics Institute in Copenhagen could continue undisturbed under the German occupation. But then that was part and parcel of the unique German treatment of Denmark. That country Hitler thought best to treat as something of a model protectorate. Normal civilian life in Denmark went on, with few restrictions, as also the life of the king. There were, as yet, no restrictions or discriminations forced on the lives of the—not numerous—Jews living in Denmark. Undoubtedly Bohr was observed occasionally by Germans, but he was able to work and to lecture; he even sent an article to a British scientific journal. He maintained some contact with American and British colleagues, partly through Sweden, partly through the remaining American legation in Denmark.

Of course he followed the news of the war with great anxiety and concern. But he did not heard directly from Heisenberg until September 1941—a condition that must have been an element in his mind when his former friend and student appeared in Copenhagen, rather surprisingly, rather suddenly.

Heisenberg arrived in Copenhagen early on September 16, a Tuesday morning, having taken the night train with a sleeper from Berlin. He took a room in a tourist hotel. That very night he walked through the city to Bohr's house. That was the first of his three visits to Bohr and his wife. He left Copenhagen on Sunday the twenty-first.

The subject or focus of the new accumulated (and perhaps still growing) mass of books and papers and records of their meetings is the question (or riddle, or conundrum) of what happened between Heisenberg and Bohr in Copenhagen. Narrowing the focus further: What had Heisenberg said to Bohr? Or, even more accurately, what had Bohr heard him say? Heisenberg wrote in *his* published reminiscences (as did his wife in hers) about their meeting in general terms; Bohr, whose attention and, consequently, whose recollections were more acute than Heisenberg's, spoke about it to those close to him; and later, when a public controversy was about to emerge, wrote letters to Heisenberg, still extant, even though Bohr chose not to send them after all. In 2001, Bohr's descendants and the Bohr Archive in Copenhagen decided to make these drafts and letters public. These papers did not reveal much that was startlingly new. However, they confirmed Bohr's shock (a shock, more than a disappointment) with what Heisenberg had said to him in September 1941.

Now during those five days and evenings in Copenhagen, Heisenberg and Bohr met often, not only in Bohr's home but also among other physicists in Bohr's institute; and then there was their now famous after-dinner walk, probably on

Wednesday night the seventeenth. Their topics were the war, as it was or seemed at that time, and then, it seems only once, the prospect of the potential making of an atomic explosive. I believe—this being the purpose of this chapter—that these two themes were inseparable; indeed, that Bohr's bitter disappointments issued from Heisenberg's statements about the first even more than about the second.

The controversy, or Bohr's possible understanding or misunderstanding of Heisenberg's intentions, was, and remains, inseparable from the actual conditions of Heisenberg's visit to Copenhagen. It seems that the very idea of his visit to Copenhagen came from C. F. von Weizsaecker. This *is* significant and deserves some explanation. Weizsaecker was in Berlin and Heisenberg in Leipzig, but they had become close friends in the late 1930s and thereafter. And colleagues too: in the summer of 1940, Weizsaecker, on the spur of the moment, came up with a brilliant idea concerning nuclear particles. More important, his father, Ernst von Weizsaecker, state secretary in the German Foreign Ministry, was second only to Ribbentrop. He was of the older type of German diplomatist, not a convinced or even committed Nazi: Ribbentrop knew this but kept him on (so did Hitler, indeed to the very end: late in the war he appointed Weizsaecker to the post of German ambassador to the Holy See in Rome).[7] He wished Hitler were more prudent (he wrote a memorandum in April 1941 warning against a war in Russia); but he also wished that the Third Reich would win the war; surely he did not want Germany to lose it. In the 1920s he had been German minister to Denmark. It was through his recommendation and assistance that Heisenberg's journey to Copenhagen was arranged.

Academics and scholars will, or ought to, admit that often the main intention of meeting a particular friend or friends may be facilitated through the pretext of a conference, enabling them thus to meet. It seems that the original idea of Heisenberg's Copenhagen visit was Weizsaecker's. Weizsaecker had gone to Copenhagen already in March 1941, when he met Bohr. His and Heisenberg's main intentions were to meet Bohr and to talk to and with him. The occasion was to be an astrophysical conference in Copenhagen arranged by the German Scientific Institute, an institution established by the Third Reich. Two other German academics went to Copenhagen too. There were to be lectures, including one by Heisenberg, in that institute—where, except for the occasion of Heisenberg's lecture, many Danish physicists declined to appear.[8] There were more get-togethers and lunches in Bohr's institute. On one occasion Heisenberg spoke in Danish.

There is some evidence that before Heisenberg's arrival in Copenhagen, Bohr, and especially his wife, Margarethe, hesitated whether to invite Heisenberg to their house to dinner. They were uneasy with Heisenberg—in a way in which their Jewish colleagues in America had been suspicious of him in 1939, and probably also because of the silence from Heisenberg ever since the German occupation of Denmark;[9] even more probably, because they were unsure of what Heisenberg planned to do and how he would behave once in Copenhagen. But these hesitations soon dissipated. After all, Niels Bohr wanted to see Werner Heisenberg; Heisenberg contacted Bohr immediately after his arrival and well before the opening of the conference; on his first day he walked across the city late in the evening to get to the Bohrs.'

Neither of them had planned to discuss politics, which of course meant the war; but those intentions melted away fast. Already at the lunches and discussions in Bohr's institute, Heisenberg talked about the war, in the presence of others. His—repeated—statements shocked and impressed Bohr. On at least two occasions Heisenberg said that Germany was winning the war—indeed, that Germany was close to winning it at that time. On another occasion Heisenberg stiffly refuted statements by Bohr and others about the German treatment and behavior of occupied countries such as Poland.

It is at least possible that Heisenberg's statements at these meetings—he knew that he could be observed by some people of the German secret services—were meant to protect himself in view of the powers in Berlin. But then his remarks about the war in the institute did not differ much from how he was talking privately in Bohr's home during and after their dinners. Moreover, yes, Bohr was permitted to live and work physically and professionally a largely free life in Hitler's model Danish protectorate; and to Heisenberg it seemed that, under the circumstances, this was perhaps enough. He could not or did not comprehend the depressing mental conditions of Bohr's life, of a half-Jewish scientist in German-occupied Denmark. Had he understood that better, he might have approached Bohr somewhat differently.

I shall yet return to Heisenberg's view of the war, but before that I must attempt to disentangle—necessarily imperfectly—the other, though related, matter between himself and Bohr: that of the prospect of atomic bombs. It is hardly questionable that a talk with Bohr about *that* topic was *the* main intention of Weizsaecker (and of Heisenberg) in arranging the trip to Copenhagen. Heisenberg brought up the problem or question of the prospect of atomic bombs only once, during their private walk and talk. That night Heisenberg spoke most of the time; Bohr, listening closely, was reticent. He was nervous and (understandably) suspicious. It seems that the talk, again, began with politics; that Heisenberg said that he believed Soviet Russia would soon be defeated, which was a good thing. He then said something about his and Weizsaecker's contacts with the German legation in Copenhagen, attempting to ensure that Bohr would be protected from interference with his person and his work; it seems that he proposed that it would be useful and desirable if Bohr would have some contact with the German legation. Then Heisenberg asked Bohr whether he understood, too, that now, after the successful fission experiments, atomic bombs could be made. This included a suggestion that this could (rather than would) be achieved in Germany and the war, if it lasted long enough, could be waged by atomic weapons. Then he seems to have made an even more oblique suggestion about how good it would be if perhaps physicists on both sides of the war (meaning the German war against the West) could refrain from working toward atomic weapons. Bohr's reactions to what Heisenberg was saying were bleakly negative. Heisenberg told that to Weizsaecker immediately after he returned to his hotel; he said that Bohr did not understand him and that their talk was a failure.

Bohr seems to have thought that Heisenberg brought up the suggestion that the making of a German nuclear bomb was a possibility with the intention of impressing him. Heisenberg seems to have thought that because of Bohr's potential and perhaps even actual contacts with physicists in Allied countries, some kind of a tacit agreement might be attempted to avoid making bombs. Bohr thought that such a secret agreement across the world was nonsense; in this Bohr was right. He also thought that Heisenberg may have been somehow attempting to frighten or even blackmail him with the suggestion that the making of an atomic bomb was after all possible in Germany too; in this Bohr was wrong.

The main documentary sources of this conversation are in the drafts of Bohr's letters to Heisenberg in 1957 that he then chose not to send. The origin of these unsent letters was Bohr's angry reaction to a book published in 1956, written by Robert Jungk (*Brighter than a Thousand Suns*); Jungk proposed that while in America scientists were producing atomic bombs, in Germany Heisenberg and others had refused to do so. Ten years before that, in 1947, Heisenberg had visited Bohr in Copenhagen; they also met later, the last time in 1961 (Bohr died in 1962). Bohr was courteous to Heisenberg and later somewhat mellowed; but their prewar close friendship was not reborn.

There exists yet another document, recently found and made available by Heisenberg's family,[10] after the opening of the Bohr Archive. It is a long letter that Heisenberg wrote in Copenhagen on three evenings to his wife, mailed in Berlin after his return. Since it reveals much of Heisenberg's then views of his war as well as of how he saw Bohr, I must cite it in some detail.

He wrote the first portion of it probably on Wednesday the seventeenth (it may have been wrongly dated as the sixteenth, Tuesday, subsequently by his wife). It begins with an account of his train travel and with his sentimental revisiting of Copenhagen, with its churches and bells. "Late [last] night I walked under a clear and starry sky across the city, darkened, to Bohr. Bohr and his family are doing fine; he has aged a little. His sons are fully grown now. The conversation quickly turned to the human concerns and unhappy events of these times: about the human affairs the consensus is given; in questions of politics I find it difficult that even a man like Bohr can not separate out thinking, feeling, and hating entirely." Then something about Mrs. Bohr and children. "Later I was sitting for a long time with Bohr alone; it was after midnight when he accompanied me to the streetcar, together with Hans [Bohr]." He added another portion to the letter Thursday night. "Yesterday I was again with Bohr for the whole evening; aside from Mrs. Bohr and the children, there was a young English woman, taken in by the Bohrs, because she can not return to England.[11] It is somewhat weird to talk with an English woman these days. During the unavoidable political conversations, where it naturally and automatically became my assigned part to defend our system, she retired, and I thought that was actually very nice of her." Next morning, with Weizsaecker, "we ate a meal on the Langelinie, all around us there were essentially only happy, cheerful people, at least it appeared that way to us. In general, people look so happy here. At night in the streets one sees all these radiantly happy young couples!" "In Bohr's Institute we had some scientific discussions, the Copenhagen group, however, doesn't know much more than we do either. Tomorrow the talks in the German Scientific Institute are beginning, the first official talk is mine, tomorrow night. Sadly the members of Bohr's Institute will not attend for political reasons. It is amazing, given that the Danes are living totally unrestricted, and are living exceptionally well, how much hatred or fear has been galvanized here, so that even a rapprochement in the cultural arena . . . has become almost impossible . . . nobody wants to go to the German Scientific Institute on principle."[12] "Today I was once more, with Weizsaecker, at Bohr's. In many ways this was especially nice, the conversation revolved for a large part of the evening around purely human concerns. Bohr was reading aloud. I played a Mozart sonata (A-Major)." "On the way home the night sky was again star-studded."

Heisenberg made no mention of or even a suggestion about his nocturnal walk and talk with Bohr, and nothing about the subject of nuclear prospects in this letter to his wife, mailed in Berlin; nothing, either, in his report to the German Ministry of Education that he wrote immediately after his return to Leipzig. Yet the main intention of both Weizsaecker and Bohr in arranging this Copenhagen journey, including the conference, was to establish contact and perhaps some kind of arrangement with Bohr. That intention was primarily political. They could not expect much technical information or scientific advice from Bohr, who—as we have seen—had been more skeptical about the prospect of an eventual construction of atomic weapons than Heisenberg and others; and who was both older and less energetic than Heisenberg and other younger physicists. They knew, too, that, even under the German occupation of Denmark, Bohr had possibilities of contact with other colleagues on the other side of the war, not only in or through Sweden but even to England and the United States.

That atomic bombs could be made, and that eventually they could change the course and the result of the war, was knowledge current among the leaders of the Third Reich, including Hitler, Goebbels, and some of their top generals. That, at a very important conference in June 1942, Heisenberg said to Hitler's top armament minister, Speer, that an atomic bomb could be made but that its construction would take a long time and require immense efforts and expenditures is now well known. According to some people this proves that Heisenberg took a stand against making a bomb for Hitler; according to others Heisenberg's continuing work on building a nuclear reactor proves simply that he and his Germans were unable to build one. Both arguments are exaggerations. It was not until the last months of the war that Americans learned that Heisenberg and the Germans were not building a bomb. And why? "Intentions," as Samuel Johnson said, "must be gathered from acts." True—even though (as also in the nature of subatomic particles) actuality is hardly separable from potentiality. During the war, many refugee physicists in America thought that Heisenberg was both able and willing to support the building of a German atomic bomb. The Austrian and originally Jewish Lise Meitner, a very good scientist, who knew Heisenberg well before she fled Germany in 1938,[13] wrote in 1945 that "the way [Heisenberg] turned up in Denmark in 1941 is unforgettable."[14] Einstein, in a remark written well after the war, said that Heisenberg was "a big Nazi."[15] That was nonsense and, perhaps worse than nonsense: untrue.

Closer to the truth, there was a duality in Heisenberg's mind, a duality that existed and still exists in the minds of many of his countrymen. He did not want Germany to lose the war. At the same time he regretted the war—the war against the West.[16] One important, though indirect, evidence of this is the message that Heisenberg's colleague Fritz Houtermans chose to give, bravely, to Fritz Reiche, an engaging and modest Jewish physicist who as late as March 1941 had received a visa and an exit permit to the United States. "Please remember [there] to tell the interested people the following thing. We are trying here hard, including Heisenberg, to hinder the idea of making a bomb. But the pressure from above . . . Please say all this: that Heisenberg will not be able to withstand longer the pressure from the government to go very earnestly and seriously into the making of the bomb."[17] Note, however, that this happened before Heisenberg's visit to Copenhagen, and before the German war against Russia.

There are more than dualities; there are many motives as well as purposes within human intentions and actions. We cannot exactly know—and perhaps neither Heisenberg *nor* Bohr could exactly know—what was the exact purpose of Heisenberg's mention of the potentiality of a German bomb to Bohr. But we may be fairly sure that at least one of them included his knowledge of Bohr's—actual as well as potential—contacts with Allied physicists through Sweden or otherwise,[18] contacts that somehow continued until Bohr's flight from Denmark in 1943.

Ambiguity and ambivalence: they may overlap but they are not the same. It may be argued that Heisenberg's inclinations involving a German-made bomb were ambiguous. Had he been told: "No matter how long and expensive the effort. Go ahead"—would he have declined or sabotaged the plan? Probably not; but at the same time it is also probable that Speer's response, effectively not to go ahead, gave him a sense of relief. In any event, he went on working on the making of a nuclear reactor. He said, several times during the war, even close to its end, that he did not wish that Germany would lose it; he did not want Germany to be defeated, though he did not wish the National Socialist Third Reich to be victorious. But then, sadly until the very end, Germany and the National Socialist Third Reich were not separable—except in his mind and in the minds of many millions of other Germans.

That was ambiguity, rather than ambivalence. His mind (and, again, that of many millions of other Germans) was marked, rather, by an ambivalence. He regretted Germany's war against the West, but supported the German war against

Russia, the Soviet Union. There are evidences of his regret of the first: among them his respect for the young Englishwoman in Bohr's house in Copenhagen (in his letter to his wife), and in a letter to his mother in November 1940 about Chamberlain's death. "There [in England] verily a nation keeps fighting and one must really admire how much people in London are able to bear?"[19] These were not the words—and sentiments—of a "Nazi."

Again—as in the minds of many other Germans—his ambivalence was part and parcel of his anti-Communism. A sharp memory of his early youth was the brief "Soviet" episode in Munich in 1919. He voiced his contempt for, and fear and hatred of, Communism often; in August 1939 his reaction to the first rumors of a German pact with the Soviet Union was one of incredulity. And now we come to September 1941 and his statements in Copenhagen,[20] at the time when the German armies were racing ahead in Russia, encircling Leningrad, ready to break into Kiev, closer and closer every day to Moscow; when the Soviet Union (as Stalin himself admitted to Churchill in early September) "was on the verge of collapse." As late as 1944 he would say: "Must we hope that we lose the war?" The year before, visiting Holland, he told a Dutch physicist that it has "always been the mission of Germany to defend the West and its culture against the onslaught of eastern hordes . . . and so, perhaps, a Europe under Germany leadership might be the lesser evil."[21]

Heisenberg's wishes and his purposes in Copenhagen were not wholly different from those of Rudolf Hess, who a few months before had taken upon himself the task of flying to Britain to attempt to persuade the British to make peace or at least an armistice with Germany. In their different ways both Hess and Heisenberg regretted the war between Germany and Britain (with America coming closer and closer to the British side). Both thought that Germany was winning: Hess shortly before the German invasion of Russia, Heisenberg (with even more reason) after that. Both of them thought in terms of the Two-War Idea.

What was—and still is—the German Two-War Idea? It is that Germany fought two wars: one against the Western democracies, the Anglo-American side, the other against Russia, the incarnation of Communism; that one was regrettable and avoidable, while the other was not; regrettable, too, was the fact that Germany's Anglo-American opponents did not understand this. Appearances and attractions of the Two-War Idea persist even now. They were at the bottom of the *Historikerstreit*, the historians' controversy of 1986; and they are stated and promoted by certain Germans (and also by some British "revisionists") to this day.

There is plenty of evidence that the Two-War Idea accorded with German sentiments as well as with German political calculations in 1941. It was there in the dreadful difference in the treatment of Western and Russian prisoners of war: one million of the latter were starved to death in German prison compounds in 1941. It was there among respectable non-Nazis such as Heisenberg, the most telling example being that of Archbishop (later Cardinal) Clemens August von Galen, who, from his pulpit in Münster in August 1941, attacked the Nazi practice of euthanasia and who, in the same sermon, praised the invasion of Russia as a crusade against atheistic Communism. (Hitler chose to leave Galen alone.) Such a duality, or ambivalence, was there in Heisenberg's mind, too. At the same time, what he and Weizsaecker were trying to do in Copenhagen was something more intricate than the duality of that archbishop and the intention of Hess. After all, Heisenberg was attempting to contact not a British duke but an old friend, a Danish physicist; and there was both naïveté and idealism in his attempt to suggest something to Allied physicists by way of Bohr. At the same time his attempt was not at all devoid of political considerations and calculations.

After all, the German government supported Heisenberg's mission. However, *German government* is an imprecise term. The government of the Third Reich was both autocratic and polycratic. Some of its organs, some of its people, had different inclinations. There was the Abwehr; there was the Gestapo; there was the foreign minister and men such as Weizsaecker's father; there was the *SS*; there were Canaris, Ribbentrop, Himmler, different men. Different, yes, but the Two-War Idea, in some ways, was shared by all of them, and by the German people at large. And a consequence of the Two-War Idea was that of multiple German attempts—including not a few approved by Hitler—to split the, to them, unnatural coalition of British and Americans and Russians.

The German regime (or at least some members of it) knew of Bohr's contacts abroad; that Bohr corresponded with Allied scientists through Sweden (including a principal British physicist, Sir James Chadwick). I am not saying that they had access to that kind of clandestine correspondence. (In one instance they did.) But they, for political reasons, allowed a relative measure of private freedoms in Denmark, where Bohr, too, went on living and working, though under dark clouds and surveillance, until he fled to Sweden and therefrom to Britain in 1943. I am not saying that they facilitated Bohr's escape to the Allies. I am saying that in 1941 they thought it to be in their interest to permit the existence of certain indirect contacts with the Western Allies, since they saw at least potential advantages in such. That was their, more than occasional, practice throughout the rest of the war.

Heisenberg's purposes and his failure to come close to a meeting of minds with Bohr in Copenhagen were complicated. The "uncertainties" of what happened then were historical, personal, national, and political—as were the "causes" of the atomic bomb.

Had only Germans and British not fought each other (in 1940 or 1941 or thereafter): this was the wish (and often the daydream) of many "conservatives," not only in Germany but throughout Europe, for many of them till this day. That would have allowed the Germans to clean up Russia and Communism; and so what? At the bottom of this wish (but not very deep down) was and is the belief that Communism and Russia were more dangerous (and more evil) than were National Socialism and Germany. That is a half-truth. But half-truths are more dangerous—and enduring—than are lies.

Four

Necessary Evil

Patrick Buchanan's book *Churchill, Hitler, and the Unnecessary War: How Britain Lost Its Empire and the West Lost the World* contains two themes under one cover. One is addressed to the present, the other to the Second World War. One is his declaration that the American empire is in great and deep trouble—that, like the British Empire two-thirds of a century ago, it is overextended and weak. The other is that the Second World War was a grievous mistake—that Britain (foremost Churchill) and America should not have fought Hitler's Germany. The two themes are not equivalent, and their treatment in this book is uneven. The vast majority of pages are about World War II. But in Buchanan's mind, the two themes are obviously inextricable, indeed, dependent on each other. For the purpose of a review, however, I must separate them.

That the present American empire is much overextended, overgrown, and at risk of all kinds of dangers, most of them willfully ignored by the American people and their politicians, is so. Buchanan deserves credit for having pointed this out, again and again, in his articles and books. But, alas, in his discussion of his larger thesis, his arguments are stamped by what we might call selective indignation or, more accurately, special pleading. (Indignation, after all, is almost always selective, while not every pleading is necessarily special.)

He claims that the transformation of the United States from a republic to an empire was started by George W. Bush. What Bush did is, of course, lamentable. But the reaching out of American power all over the world, the fact that there are now American bases and missions in more than eight hundred places around the globe, the building of a six-hundred-ship navy, etc., began with Eisenhower and Dulles. It went on with Johnson, Nixon, Carter, and especially with Buchanan's hero Reagan, and then under Clinton. Already in 1956, Section Nine of the Republican Party platform called for "the establishment of American air and navy bases all around the world." This was the party that so many liberal commentators still wrongly called "isolationist." This was the party to which Patrick Buchanan adhered and the American foreign policy he vocally thumped for until very recently.

The other trouble with Buchanan's anti-imperialist thesis is his argument that what happened to the British Empire applies obviously to the present American one. There are two points against this. One is that history does not repeat itself, and the rise and decline of Britain's empire was and remains quite different from the American situation. Buchanan's argument is that the Second World War—more precisely, Churchill's decision to resist Hitler, no matter what the cost—

was a disaster for Western civilization but, more directly, for the British Empire itself. Yet the gradual liquidation of the British Empire, and the piecemeal acceptance by the British people of that, long preceded World War II.

The further and perhaps deeper problem is Buchanan's sincerity. Since when has he been an admirer of the British Empire? There is no evidence for such an affection in his public or writing career until now. To the contrary, there is ample evidence of his conviction that the United States should not have supported Britain and its empire either in the First or in the Second World War.

Here I arrive at the main theme of this book. *How Britain Lost Its Empire and the West Lost the World* is only its subtitle, its main title being *Churchill, Hitler, and the Unnecessary War.* This emphasis accords with what is—and has been for a long time—Buchanan's view of history. The Second World War was an unnecessary war; a wrong war, especially involving Europe; it was wrong to fight Hitler; and Churchill was primarily, indeed principally, responsible. A man has, or more precisely chooses, his opinions. The choice, every so often, depends on his inclinations. In this review it is not my proper business to speculate about Buchanan's inclinations. I must restrict myself to questioning his arguments.

The British decision to offer an alliance to Poland in 1939 was a hasty one, replete with unintended consequences. Partly true. Hitler did not wish to destroy the British Empire. Partly true. He did want to destroy Communism and the Soviet Union. Partly true. Churchill was a warrior; he was obsessed with the danger of German power. Partly true. Hitler wanted to expel Jews from Europe but not to exterminate them, at least not while the former policy was still possible. Again, partly true. Or in other words, true but not true enough. Here is a difference between Patrick Buchanan and David Irving. The latter employs falsehoods; Buchanan employs half-truths. But, as Thomas Aquinas once put it, "a half-truth is more dangerous than a lie."

The Second World War began in September 1939, with Hitler's armies invading Poland. Buchanan writes that the British commitment to Poland was a stupid mistake and that the Poles should not have fought Hitler. Now here is an example of a special pleader's method: selective quotation. Buchanan will quote A. J. P. Taylor when this suits him, as when Taylor wrote, "Only Danzig prevented cooperation between Germany and Poland." (Taylor was wrong: all evidence shows that what Hitler wanted was a Poland bereft of independence from Germany.) Of course Buchanan will not cite Taylor's four words describing Churchill: "The savior of England."

Let me now raise the question: What would have happened if Britain and France had allowed Hitler to conquer Poland? After that he would have gone farther east and then conquered the Soviet Union, with the acquiescence of the West. All to the good, Buchanan writes, since Communism was evil, more dangerous than German National Socialism. But there is—and there ought to be—no comparison here. Germany was part and parcel of European culture, civilization, and tradition. Russia was not. Stalin had a predecessor, Ivan the Terrible. Hitler had none. German National Socialist brutality was unprecedented. Russian brutality was not. Nationalism, not Communism, was the main political force in the twentieth century, and so it is even now. When the Third Reich collapsed in 1945, perhaps as many as ten thousand Germans killed themselves, and not all of these had been Nazis. When the Soviet Union and Communist rule in Eastern Europe collapsed in 1989, I do not know of a single Communist, whether in Russia or elsewhere, who committed suicide.

There was a consistency in Churchill's view of Europe and of the world. To him, and for Britain, there were only two alternatives: either all of Europe dominated by Germany or the eastern half of Europe dominated by Russia, and half—especially the western half—of Europe was better than none. Besides, Churchill said that the Russians could swallow Eastern Europe but not digest it and that Communism would disappear from Eastern Europe before long. If Hitler had won the war, German rule would have been much more enduring.

This is not the first of Buchanan's many expressions of his visceral and intellectual antipathy to Churchill. Irving's main method in defending Hitler is to blacken all of Hitler's opponents, foremost among them Churchill. But then he is obsessed with what is and what is not true of the Holocaust. Buchanan is not. In this book, Buchanan deprecates Hitler: in 1942 "he was absorbed in self-pity: and he was condemning his own people." On page 383: Hitler's was "an evil and odious regime." But there is a fatal contradiction in Buchanan's theses: Hitler's regime—including, one may think, its expansion—was evil, but warring against him was unnecessary and wrong. Either thesis may be argued, but not both.

Five

THE ORIGINS OF THE COLD WAR

MANY PEOPLE, INCLUDING POLITICAL "scientists" and historians, have seen and still see the "Cold War" as a consequence of World Communism. In the United States, leading "conservatives" James Burnham and William Buckley wrote that in 1917 "history changed gears." In Germany, Ernst Nolte, a historian, wrote that beginning in 1917, with the Communist revolution in Russia, the entire history of the twentieth century thereafter was that of a "European civil war." This is—they are—wrong. The Cold War was a consequence of the Second World War. Its cause was the nature of the Russian occupation of most of Eastern Europe and of eastern Germany. The words *cold war* came into existence in the United States in 1948. We may pin down the chronological limits of the "war": 1947 to 1989. In 1947, Russian and Communist rule in the eastern portion of Europe became, by and large, unconditional; in 1989 the Communist governments in Eastern Europe ceased to exist. True, the first reactions of the American government against further Communist or Russian expansion and against the aggressiveness of the Russian government began to appear a year before 1947, the ending of hostility between the American and Russian governments about two years before 1989, and the final end of Communism and the dissolution of the Soviet Union in 1991. Still, it is proper and reasonable to *fix* the frame, the duration of the Cold War, from 1947 to 1989. What remain arguable are the related questions: What was the main "cause" of the Cold War, Communism? or Russia? or both? And, if the Cold War was but a consequence of the Second World War, was that consequence necessarily inevitable?

About this matter of the origins of the Cold War this writer thinks that he must not be accused of special pleading; and he hopes that at least some of his readers will share his sense of indignation about the ideological—that is, Communism-obsessed—explanation of the Cold War and even of the Second World War. For those who think and say and write that the history of the twentieth century was governed by the epic struggle of Democracy (or Freedom) against Communism imply that the Second World War was but a secondary chapter, an interruption of the great confrontation with that evil force. But the opposite is true. The history of the twentieth century, worldwide, was marked by the two world wars. The Russian Revolutions of 1917 were a consequence of the First World War, the Cold War of the Second. There *is* no need to argue this again, except to recognize yet another unpleasant tendency, an inclination especially current among American "conservatives," to think and to assert that Communism was more evil than National Socialism. A seemingly (but only seemingly) broader-minded version *is* the one adopted by so-called liberals, the thesis that the twentieth century represented the struggle between "Democracy" and "Totalitarianism." There is no *use* to argue about that either, except perhaps to recognize that the minds of some people are broad enough to be flat.

So back to the important question: was the Cold War unavoidable at all? Was a postwar clash of interests between Soviet Russia on one side and America and Britain on the other side inevitable? Franklin Roosevelt did not think so. Winston Churchill hoped not—at least for a while. Adolf Hitler was convinced of it.

Franklin Roosevelt's decisions and thoughts and inclinations involving Russia and Communism and Stalin have been analyzed and described and categorized for more than sixty years now. According to his harsh critics, his ideas were deluded, illusionary, and shallow; according to his admirers, they were pragmatic, shrewd, and realist. There *is* truth in both kinds of assertions, but perhaps only in the *sense* of La Rochefoucauld's maxim that there *is* at least *some* truth even in what your worst enemies *say* about you. Franklin Roosevelt's character was complex. Regarding Russia and Stalin his mind was not. He was willing to accord them a goodly amount of benevolence. The origins of that are discernible even before June 1941, that is, before Hitler's invasion of Russia. In 1933 it was his decision (long overdue) for the United States to give diplomatic recognition to the Soviet Union, establishing official state relations between these two largest states of the world.[1] Well before 1933, Roosevelt thought that most of the Republicans'

views of the world were isolationist and parochial. Not all of them were: but had a Republican such as Hoover or Taft been president of the United States in 1940, Hitler would have won the war. Roosevelt's decision to stand by Churchill and Britain at the risk of war remains to his enduring credit.

But then in 1941, Stalin and his Russia suddenly became virtual allies of Britain and of the United states. Roosevelt's first reactions to this event were cautious. He was aware of Republican and America Firster and isolationist but also of Catholic sentiments within the American people—so, unlike Churchill, he did not immediately declare an American alliance with the Soviet Union upon the news of its invasion by Hitler. But, like Churchill, Roosevelt welcomed this new turn in the war. Less than two months after the start of the German war in Russia he wrote a message to the pope, Pius XII, suggesting that the Holy See reconsider its categorical condemnation of the Soviets and of their atheistic Communism—a sign or symptom of Roosevelt's thinking as well as of his politic concern with sections of American popular opinions.

But our purpose here is not a narrative survey of American-Russian relations during the Second World War. It is the question whether the clash, or conflict, or struggle between the United States and Russia could have been avoided. Roosevelt thought so. That conflicts between them would occur he knew, but he also thought that they would eventually fade away. And so, before looking at some of these conflicts that were accumulating especially toward the end of the war—whence they may be seen as early symptoms of the coming Cold War—we may as well sum up something about this president's general inclinations involving the Soviet Union and Stalin. They were threefold (or, in other words, they existed on three connected levels). One was his inclination to believe that he could charm—or, perhaps more precisely, impress and influence—Stalin with his benevolence and amiability, with his words and manners. (That was an asset that he had often employed in his domestic political relationships, with success.) The second was his consequent tendency to distance himself from Churchill, especially when Stalin was present—at times, alas, demonstrably so. (That was a tactic of the politician Roosevelt that we may lament in retrospect: it did no good, and it hurt Churchill, but also suggested that for Roosevelt the American alliance with Russia now was even more important than the alliance with Britain.) The third was Roosevelt's overall view of where and how the history of the world was moving. He saw the United States as somewhere in the middle, in the middle between Stalin and Churchill, or between the Russian and the British empires, but also between the rough pioneer Russian system moving toward an egalitarian future and the British Empire, admirable in some ways, but antiquated and backward. (That was a thorough misreading: for it was Russia, not Britain, that was backward, led by a reincarnation of someone like Ivan the Terrible—whom Churchill saw, not altogether wrongly, as a peasant tsar.) Over all of this was Roosevelt's belief—that, at least for some time, Churchill also hoped, at least to some extent—that his wartime alliances would have a lasting effect on Stalin and, consequently, on the international behavior of the Soviet Union.

There *were* some reasons for that hopeful expectation—though, as events would show, not much and not enough.

These reasons rested on Stalin's statesmanship. His ability for that ought not be dismissed easily. During the Second World War Stalin spoke and acted often not at all like a Communist revolutionary but like a Russian statesman. Well before 1939 he realized the advantages—and the inevitability—of seeing the world, and himself, thus.[2] In this he was way above and ahead of his toadies in the Politburo, including Molotov. Anthony Eden recalled to Sumner Welles (a once leading American diplomat) a conversation with Stalin, who said: "Hitler is a genius but he doesn't know when to stop." Eden: "Does anyone know when to stop?" Stalin: "I do."[3]

Added to this was Stalin's genuine respect for Roosevelt. He knew that Roosevelt had ordered huge shipments of armaments and goods for Russia soon after the German invasion. In several instances during the war he agreed with Roosevelt; on other occasions he deferred to him. Roosevelt took hope and encouragement from Stalin's statement to Churchill's envoy Beaverbrook in October 1941 that the Soviet Union's alliance with the United States and Britain "should be extended."[4] In July 1942 he consented to Roosevelt's request to divert forty American bombers destined for Russia to the British army badly pressed in western Egypt. In November 1942, in answer to Roosevelt's apologetic explanations about having had to deal with Admiral Darlan, the former Vichy-ite commander in North Africa, Stalin wrote that Roosevelt's policy was "perfectly correct."[5] In that month Roosevelt's special envoy, General Patrick Hurley, reported to Roosevelt that "Stalin's attitude was uniformly good-natured, his expressions were always clear, direct and concise. His attitude toward you and the United States was always friendly and respectful."[6] Of course Stalin knew what Roosevelt wanted to hear, and also what the president wanted from him (for Russia to enter the war against Japan, and the Soviet Union's willingness to enter the United Nations; the first promise was made at Teheran, the second at Yalta). Still, Stalin was genuinely shocked by the sudden news of Roosevelt's death on April 12, 1945. He overruled Molotov, ordering him to proceed to Washington and to the United Nations' San Francisco Conference. The next day

Soviet newspapers carried the news of Roosevelt's death on their front pages, surrounded by black borders.

At the same time the first serious symptoms of a potential conflict with the Soviet Union already existed. But before describing some of them, I must correct the legend, assiduously disseminated by Roosevelt's admirers, that shortly before his death he had begun to change, or indeed did change, his mind about Stalin, ready to oppose the latter when and if he must. Churchill urged him to do so, but in vain. On April 11, 1945, the day before he died, the tired and wan Roosevelt at Warm Springs did dictate an often cited sentence in a message to Churchill: "We must be firm, however, and our course thus far is correct." Yet that was but a throwaway last sentence in a dispatch whose essence was this: "I would minimize the general Soviet problem as much as possible because these problems, in one form or another, seem to arise every day and most of them straighten out." In Moscow, Averell Harriman, Roosevelt's friend and ambassador, had begun, somewhat belatedly, to have serious doubts about the Russians' behavior. That same day, April 11, Roosevelt dispatched to Harriman his last message to Stalin: "There must not, in any event, be mutual mistrust and minor misunderstandings of this character [they involved Poland] should not arise in the future."[7] Before sending it on to Stalin, Harriman suggested deletion of the word *minor*. The president's chief of staff Admiral Leahy, working in the Map Room of the White House in Washington, drafted Roosevelt's response early next morning: "I do not wish to delete the word 'minor.'" A few minutes after one o'clock—after Roosevelt had had his lunch—Leahy received Roosevelt's approval of the final text. Nine minutes later the president was struck by "a terrific pain." These were his last words. He died two hours later.

Keep in mind how during the Second World War a few

men—Hitler, Churchill, Stalin, Roosevelt—governed the history of the world. This brings us to Winston Churchill. His critics (and even some of his admirers) have written that, just as Neville Chamberlain had failed to understand Hitler, Churchill had failed to understand Stalin. That parallel will not run. Chamberlain, until September 1939, had his illusions about Hitler and Germany. Churchill had few illusions about Stalin and Russia. He did not think that Stalin was an international revolutionary. Churchill thought that the best way to avoid, or at least limit, coming conflicts with Stalin and Russia was to agree on a more or less precise definition of the geographical extent of Russia's sphere of interest before the end of the war. Because of Roosevelt's opposition, Churchill did not have his way. After 1943 his prestige was still great, but his and Britain's power were not. He, too, was tired and worn; he tried to influence the Americans, but in the end he thought it best to defer to them. His wish for a special relationship between Britain and the United States existed throughout his life. It governed, also, the last volume of his *History of the Second World War.* In 1952 he wrote in a confidential letter to Eisenhower that he chose not to recall or emphasize or even mention some of his disagreements with the Americans during the last and decisive year of the war in Europe. (That accorded with his tendency of never reminding people: "I told you so.") But it also obscured essential matters. After all, the title of his sixth volume was *Triumph and Tragedy.* That word *tragedy* did not occur to any American or Russian after the war. The tragedy was the division of Europe, and the coming of a Cold War. The astonishing acuity of Churchill's vision was recounted not by himself but by General De Gaulle in his *Memoirs.* In November 1944, De Gaulle, trying to coax Churchill away from the Americans, said that they were shortsighted and inexperienced, allowing vast portions of Eastern Europe to fall to the Russians. Churchill said, yes, that was so. "Russia is now a hungry wolf amidst a flock of sheep. But after the meal comes the digestion period." Russia would not be able to digest all of her Eastern European conquests. That was so—but only in the long run. Before that the Cold War arose.

Of that eventuality Adolf Hitler was convinced. Much of his strategy and policy was inspired by what he saw as an irrepressible conflict between the Anglo-Americans and the Russians. Before the end of the war he spoke of this to his confidants on many occasions. He saw, or at least pretended to see, the first signs of such a conflict, even the prospect of a clash of arms, from which he and Germany would profit. But his time was running out. He killed himself on April 30, 1945. Five days before that, American and Russian troops met and shook hands in the middle of Germany, near Torgau on the Elbe, a symbolic event of a division of Europe not far from Wittenberg—where more than four hundred years before Luther had made his declaration, whereafter Germany and Christendom became divided.

A book summing up the episodes and attempts with which Hitler's regime tried to divide the Allied coalition after 1941 remains to be written. Its author will have a difficult task. There were many such attempts; he will have to distinguish between serious and not-so-serious, subtle and not-so-subtle ones; he will have to comprehend not only the intricacies of the different personnel within the regime of the Third Reich but also something about their Allied counterparts; and he ought to surmise at least some things about Hitler's knowledge of these attempts. I can and must do not much more than a summary sketch here (or call it "Suggestions for further research"), subordinated to the question about the origins of the Cold War. For Hitler's main purpose—and that of other Germans, understandably so—was not only to cause suspicions and frictions between the British and the Americans and the Russians but to help bring about actual conflicts between them.

Hitler thought and often said to his subordinates and to people who urged him to seek contact with one or another of his adversaries that such a political move had to be preceded by a resounding German military victory in the field, on one front or another. More than one of his most important military decisions he took with that in mind: the battle of Kursk in July 1943 and the last German offensive in Belgium in December 1944, for example. His rationale for these endeavors exists in the record of his own words. Apart from that he put not much faith in diplomatic or political or other clandestine attempts. Not much, but some. He seldom encouraged such, but he did not always discourage them. His consent to such operations, or moves, was seldom explicit; more often it was implicit, in one way or another. That was the case with the several attempts that Heinrich Himmler made, establishing some contact with the services of the Western Allies in several circumstances and on several occasions. It is ever so: often the head of the secret services of a state who, no matter how cruel or brutal his record, knows the prospects of defeat and tries to contravene them: such was the case of Fouché near the end of Napoleon, of Beria after the death of Stalin, and of Heinrich Himmler in 1944 and 1945. His underlings' negotiations with certain Jewish persons in Hungary in 1944, their contact with Americans later in that year, their negotiations with Raoul Wallenberg, again in Hungary near the end of 1944, were promoted for the main purpose of making trouble among the Allies, and preferably between Americans and Russians. Some of them may have been undertaken behind Hitler's back, but not without Hitler's knowledge, and (until the very last days of the war) not against Hitler's wishes.

The most important of such contacts occurred in Italy in 1944 and 1945. In one instance Hitler preceded Himmler. He ordered that the German evacuation of Rome should take place without any damage to the Eternal City; and he suggested to General Kesselring that he try to establish contacts with American generals before or during the German withdrawal. That did not happen; but more important were the—not at all unconditional—surrender negotiations between the *SS* General Karl Wolff and the mostly American (with some British) representatives in Italy and Switzerland beginning in January 1945, negotiations that not only Himmler but also Hitler knew about and allowed, implicitly as well as explicitly at times. Wolff and Himmler could take at least some satisfaction from these protracted negotiations. They certainly rattled and irritated Stalin, leading to a short but bitter exchange of messages between him and Roosevelt in early April 1945.[8] The contacts began with the help of an Italian middleman, Parilli, who thought that certain Germans "had hoped eventually to fight together with [the Americans] against the Russians." "The thought of dividing the Western Allies from the Russians was the last great hope of the German leadership and ran like a red thread through all of the negotiations." Thus two months before Hitler's suicide, American generals and an *SS* general sat at the same table in Switzerland. (On April 15, Wolff wrote a letter to Allen Dulles, expressing his condolences on President Roosevelt's death.) The next day, April 16, Himmler—and Hitler—ordered Wolff (the order was repeated three times) to Berlin, where he spent more than ten hours with Himmler and the *SS* chief Kaltenbrunner before seeing Hitler. Next day (the seventeenth) Hitler received Wolff and, in his way, wished him well in his endeavor. He did tell him to perhaps wait a bit before signing an armistice with the Americans, but he still "saw in [these negotiations] a good instrument to cause dissensions within the anti-Hitler coalition." He said to Wolff that the German armies may be fighting for another two months. "During these two decisive months of the war a break . . . between the Russians and the Anglo-Saxons will come, and whichever of the two sides comes to him, he will gladly ally with them against the other."[9]

Here we must understand that, at least about these matters, Hitler and his subordinates and the majority of the German people were largely in accord. The German people hoped to be dealt better by the Americans than by the Russians (and also than by the English). That was understandable. They had every reason to think and believe that the Americans would treat them with no sentiments of revenge, with less hatred and savagery than the Russians, whom they feared. That was why during the last three months of the war the German armies retreated faster and fought less determinedly along the Western than on the Eastern Front. There were hundreds of episodes when the German population accepted with some relief the American troops overrunning and occupying. There was, too, an element of opportunism in the expectations of the German population about the Americans. The excellent German historian of the American occupation of Germany Henke noted "the astonishing optimism of the [west German] industrial elite" during the first weeks of the American occupation, asserting "business as usual," making references in favor of Americans (and of course to the savagery of Russians). But also against the British: as early as April 1945 some of the Krupp executives asked the Americans to support them against a British commission due to arrive. One of their leaders said to the Americans: "The British want nothing else but the destruction of German industrial competition." No matter how correctly the British occupiers behaved, Germans expected nothing from them but cold contempt; they saw them (but not the Americans) as rigid and determined enemies.[10] But that had little or nothing to do with the origins of the Cold War.

What were the first symptoms of the Cold War? While keeping in mind that an early symptom does not necessarily result in a protracted crisis, we ought to consider them, at least cursorily. We must also keep in mind the difference, and the time elapsed, between the diagnosis of a symptom and its treatment—and the ability or the inability (which so often suggests the willingness or the unwillingness) to recognize the meaning of the symptom. About this there was a decisive difference between Roosevelt and Churchill. The American inclination was to get on with and through the war: political problems, including peace settlements, must come later. Churchill thought and wrote—even in his toned-down memoir *Triumph and Tragedy*—that, especially toward the end of a great war, military and political decisions cannot be considered separately: "At the summit they are one." He did not have *his* way.

There were reasons for that American attitude: the continuing war against Japan and the hope of Russian participation in it; and the still existing isolationism among many Americans, wishing to end the war in Europe and to bring

Americans home as soon as possible. These explain much of the general American unwillingness to confront problems with Stalin and the Soviet Union before the end of the war in Europe and, indeed, for some time thereafter.

Yet—a perhaps pardonable generalization—whereas in science the rules count, in history exceptions may or may not rule but noticed they must be. There was the overall, and often overwhelming, American inclination to brush problems with Russia under the rug (or indeed not to note them at all); but there *were* some signs of an American concern with the Soviet Union and with its potential projects in Europe as the Russian armies were pouring westward. And here any thoughtful historian must at least try to look at the complex nature of what was "American," including "Washington," that is, "the government." Consider only two very different persons in the Roosevelt government, in 1944 and 1945. One was Henry Morgenthau, the secretary of the treasury, a confidant and country neighbor of Franklin Roosevelt, a man who was constantly exaggerating his importance, asserting his closeness to the president, which was not really so. Yet he had his way, at times in important matters. He was the author and propagator of the Morgenthau Plan, aimed at the permanent demolition of Germany's industrial capacity, reducing Germany to hardly more than agriculture. Roosevelt (and even Churchill) accepted that in September 1944, without paying much attention to it; a few months later Morgenthau's plan was ignored and dropped by the different military and other American policy makers in occupied Germany, but still . . . Another person was Allen Dulles, chief of the secret Office of Strategic Services in Switzerland, whom we met at the instance of his palavers with Wolff, the *SS* general; but Dulles was involved in other negotiations, too, with other non-Nazi Germans. His principal aim was the very opposite of Morgenthau's proposed treatment of Germany. Dulles was concerned about preventing a destroyed Germany, a perilous vacuum of a great state whose leaders would be predominantly pro-Russian. He had at least some reasons to be concerned about that: Stalin had already permitted the formation of a committee of German nationalist generals, a possible nucleus of a postwar German regime. It is not clear why Roosevelt chose Dulles to be his—less and less clandestine—representative in Switzerland: but there Dulles was and remained.[11] Meanwhile, there were a few signs of Roosevelt's concern with Western Europe. His dislike of De Gaulle was connected with the American concern over undue Communist influences in a liberated France, whereto all kinds of clandestine American intelligence agents were sent in August and September 1944. On one occasion (at or before Teheran) Roosevelt sketched the—impractical—design of a narrow American corridor leading to a Russian-occupied Berlin; but that was before the tripartite discussions and agreements about the zoning of Germany came about in 1944 and 1945.

In any event—it was not simply Roosevelt's unwillingness to disagree with Stalin that ultimately led to a rigid division of Europe and to the Cold War. A—connected—factor was Roosevelt's lack of interest in Eastern Europe. That was why he was satisfied at Yalta with the imprecise and generally meaningless Declaration of Liberated Europe to which Stalin there agreed (Molotov was seen mumbling to Stalin, warning against its phrasing). That was why Roosevelt, contrary to Churchill, did not want to argue or to even make an issue about Poland with Stalin. There were, too, signs in the United States, mutterings by Republicans and a few congressmen as early as 1944, concerned about the demolition of Germany to

the ultimate advantage of Russia. These rumblings were not yet influential, but they were noticed by intelligent foreign observers.[12]

Churchill was more concerned with Eastern Europe than was Roosevelt—and not only because he felt that Britain owed something to a heroic and tragic Poland. He knew the history and the geography of Europe: he was concerned with Austria, Hungary, Czechoslovakia, rather than with Romania and Bulgaria. The last two had been often dependent on imperial Russia, while the others belonged to Central, rather than Eastern, Europe (As late as December 1944 he wrote to Roosevelt about that distinction.) But his powers were limited—not only in regard to Roosevelt but in regard to Stalin, too, because of their Percentages Agreement, which Stalin, especially about Greece, fulfilled exactly. When in December 1944 Churchill sent British troops to Athens to help crush a Communist uprising there, Stalin kept to their agreement and did nothing.[13] At the same time the State Department and the American press assailed Churchill's intervention in Greece.

Much of this would change after Yalta. But before that we must look at what were early symptoms of Russian hostility and of Russian suspicions of their Western allies. There were of course many of them. Until D-Day Stalin was both vexed with and suspicious of the slow progress of the Anglo-Americans toward opening up a real Second Front in Western Europe. He feared that Churchill did not want a great invasion of France at all (he had at least some reasons for his suspicions). He was irritated by not having been informed about the American negotiations with Italians before Italy's surrender in 1943, and thereafter by some of the difficulties in transferring Italian warships that had been promised to the Soviet Union. In 1942 and 1943, Roosevelt and Churchill had to consider the danger of a separate peace or armistice between Stalin and Hitler. Stalin did not much fear the converse, but in January 1944 *Pravda* suddenly published an article about some British and German personalities meeting in Madrid about a separate peace. That was entirely untrue; Churchill protested to Stalin. All of this occurred before Yalta.

Was Stalin preparing for an unavoidable conflict with the Capitalist Powers as early as 1944? We cannot tell. What we must keep in mind is a characteristic in Russian history that prevailed under such different regimes as those of Alexander I and Alexander III and then of Stalin in the 1930s and during most of the war: the discrepancy between Russia's foreign policy and its internal regime. Stalin's alliance with Britain and the United States, his acceptance and occasional cultivation of amicable relations with Churchill and Roosevelt, had hardly any consequences and no counterpart in the functioning of the Soviet police state. There there were a few, not insignificant, changes during the war: the promotion of historic symbols and names, a new national anthem, dissolution of the Comintern, open support of the Russian Orthodox Church, and so on; but these were symptoms of nationalism, not of internationalism. When George Kennan, the profoundest American student of Russia, was again posted to Moscow in 1944, he took up his pen and wrote an essay: "Russia—Seven Years Later." It was an extraordinarily perceptive analysis of what could be expected of Russia and of its foreign policy—in many ways it was a forerunner of Kennan's famous "X" article three years later—but an important part of it was Kennan's argument that the essence of the Russian police state remained the same. His essay was not read by many in Washington at that time.

Here we arrive at Yalta—at its relationship to the origins of the Cold War. More than sixty years later we have a mass of books and articles and public speeches arguing that Yalta was a failure or that it was not; again, there is some truth in both kinds of allegations. The euphoria (especially in the United States) that followed the Yalta agreements and declarations was unwarranted; yet Franklin Roosevelt had at least some reasons to think that his meeting of minds with Stalin was a great success. Stalin agreed that the Soviet Union would become part of the United Nations. He promised that Russia would enter the war against Japan three months after the end of the war with Germany. Churchill was not optimistic. His estimation of the value of a future United Nations was much lower than Roosevelt's. He still cared much about Poland—but Poland at the time of Yalta had been overrun and "liberated" by the Soviet armies. The main problem involved no longer the shape, the frontiers of a new postwar Poland; it was the composition and the character of its government, that is, the very nature of its people's lives. In the lengthy discussions about Poland, Stalin was largely adamant, Roosevelt largely bored. A kind of agreement was made, giving some leeway to a British and American presence of observation and interest in free elections due to Poland soon. There was, too, that Declaration of Liberated Europe, general and insubstantial, which Stalin interpreted in his way. He recognized the Americans' general lack of interest in Eastern Europe. He also recognized their general interest in Western Europe. The future of Germany was a different question: that was still a subject of discussions. Like Roosevelt, Stalin was not disappointed with what happened at Yalta. We may even question whether he foresaw the coming of a great conflict with the United States at that time. Yet, soon after Yalta, the first symptoms of that began to appear.

The British and the Americans soon found that there would be nothing even remotely like free elections in Poland. Stalin was irritated: on April 9 he wrote to Roosevelt that "matters in the Polish question have really reached a dead end" and offered a few insignificant concessions. He tried to inspire some trouble between Roosevelt and Churchill. In his harsh protest against the Bern negotiations with Wolff, he wrote (on April 3) to Roosevelt: "It is known that the initiative in this whole affair belonged to the British," which was not the case. He was suspicious—indeed, more than suspicious: concerned and outraged—that the Germans were surrendering in droves on the Western Front, giving up large cities "without resistance," whereas in the east, in Czechoslovakia, "they were fighting savagely . . . for some unknown [railway] junction which they need as much as a dead man needs a poultice." He *was* still worried about some kind of a Western deal with Germans.[14] When three weeks later Churchill refused Himmler's offer to capitulate only in the West, Stalin was relieved and sent an unusually effusive message of appreciation to Churchill.

Ominous symptoms were beginning to accumulate. Only a few days after V-E Day, the total German surrender, there was the imminent prospect of an armed clash between British and Commonwealth units and Tito's Communist troops attempting to break into Trieste. (Stalin warned Tito not to provoke the Western Allies there: "What is ours is ours; what is theirs is theirs.") A few weeks earlier an article was printed in a French Communist publication from the pen of a French Communist leader, Jacques Duclos, attacking the head of the

Communist Party of the United States, who during the war had instructed his party to support Roosevelt. (The significance of this article has been often exaggerated: Stalin cared not much for Duclos and his ilk.) More important, the FBI and other American secret services now had evidence that efforts were being made by Soviet agents (and especially by American Communist volunteers) to learn more and more about the making of America's secret weapon, the atomic bomb. In January 1945 Stalin and Molotov asked Washington to consider a loan of six billion dollars to a war-ravaged Russia after the end of the war: somehow this request disappeared in the bureaucratic maze of Washington (though not necessarily because of American ill will). In May and June, before the American armies in central Germany began to withdraw to the zonal boundaries agreed upon, American agents began to corral German scientists and technicians (including Wernher von Braun) in order to bring them to the United States (in some cases for the purpose of employing them in the still continuing war against Japan). After the promised Russian declaration of war against Japan and the Russian invasion against the Japanese forces on the Asian mainland had begun and Japan had surrendered, Stalin asked President Truman to allot to the Soviet Union an occupation zone, one of the four mother islands of Japan. The president of the United States refused, and Stalin had to relent.

Harry Truman's character and his view of the world were different from Franklin Roosevelt's. Yet it must not be thought that his sudden assumption of the presidency meant an instant change in America's relations with Russia—or indeed in the course of the gigantic American ship of state. True, when less than ten days after he had become president, Truman received Molotov in the White House, he spoke to this Russian in strong words to which the latter said that he was thoroughly unaccustomed. Truman's advisers instantly thought that the president's language was too harsh, and the next day Truman thought it better not to press the issue (again it was mostly Poland) with Molotov. When Churchill, a few days after the German surrender, implored Truman to take a harder line with Moscow (it was in that letter that Churchill first used the phrase *iron curtain*), Truman did not follow Churchill's urgings; another few days later he sent Joseph Davies and then Harry Hopkins to Moscow to try to iron out problems with Stalin. During the Potsdam summit meeting in July, Truman's behavior and his impressions of Stalin were still cordial and positive. Throughout 1945 (and even for two years thereafter), Truman did not altogether abandon the hope of maintaining at least acceptable relations with the Soviet Union, and particularly with Stalin.

However, he had—commendably—few or no illusions about Stalin or about Russian ambitions or about Communism. The next year, 1946, was marked by more and more troubles with Russians and Communists, involving Iran, Turkey, Greece, Yugoslavia, Berlin. In March 1946, Truman accompanied Churchill to Fulton, Missouri, where Churchill delivered his famous Iron Curtain speech (though the president and the State Department were careful to state publicly that they were not necessarily associating themselves with the former prime minister's views). By early 1947 Truman's decision was made: to oppose further Soviet advances and aggressions, to contain the Soviet Union and Communism. By that time Stalin had decided to proceed to the more or less full Communization of the countries that had fallen into his sphere of interest in Eastern Europe. There was, as yet, no sharp conflict between the Soviet Union and the United

States in China or in the Pacific. Stalin was not sure that Mao Tse-tung and his Communists could win the entire civil war in China. The Soviet Union maintained its embassy in Chungking (Chiang Kai-shek's capital) till the very end (1949). The Soviet Union did not object to the official establishment of the United States' possession or protectorate over the former Japanese islands in Micronesia (1947). But the division of Europe was about complete, and thus the Cold War began.

So let me conclude with this question: was the Cold War inevitable? One occasionally still hears a speculation: had Franklin Roosevelt lived, would the Cold War have been avoided? *That* question is senseless, because all "what if?" speculations must depend on their plausibility—and by early 1945 Roosevelt was near the threshold of his death. He and people around him did not see that, or did not wish to see that; we know it not only because of what actually happened but also from the president's medical records. On another level, had he lived, Franklin Roosevelt was politician enough to know that his protracted insistence on a cordial relationship with Stalin must not be pursued to such extent that his popularity at home would dangerously erode. He might have exacted a few concessions from Stalin, but nothing like a considerable reduction of Russia's control of Eastern Europe (and of eastern Germany).

In late 1945 slowly, gradually, American popular sentiment, and even some segments of American public opinion, were turning against Communism and the Soviet Union, mostly consequent to the news of what Communists and Russians were doing and how they were behaving in Eastern

Europe. Still, public opinion and popular sentiments were not identical. Throughout 1945 most of the public and published opinions of journalists and commentators and public personalities remained optimistic and pro-Russian, often exceedingly so. At the same time there were symptoms of increasing popular grumbling against Communism and Communists, even more than with Russia and Russians. Most of that sentiment was still inchoate, mixed up with an isolationism that had been temporarily submerged during the war. But it existed, and it was gaining strength after the end of the war. Its main ingredient was anti-Communism.[15] When in early 1947 the Truman administration took the first decisive steps toward confronting Russia, an American commitment to stand by and defend Greece and Turkey, the then assistant secretary of state Dean Acheson chose to present this to Congress by drawing a greatly exaggerated prospect of Communism and Communists spreading all over Europe.

And here, compelled as we are to deal at least with the origins of the Cold War, about which perhaps more than one hundred books have been written during the past sixty years, we need to cast a look at their two main interpretations. One of them, appearing and widespread in the 1960s, is that the American reaction to Russia in 1945 and after was too rapid and too radical. This interpretation of history, produced by historians and others mostly during the Vietnam War, projected—not very honestly—the dissatisfactions of the 1960s to what had happened twenty years before: wrongly so. The other interpretation, current mostly after the collapse of the Soviet Union, and dependent largely on the revelations of Russian and Communist intelligence machinations in and after 1945, states that the American government's reactions to the Soviet Union's deceptions and aggressiveness was just and taken at the right time. Of these two different interpretations this second is much closer to the truth: but not quite. There is—or ought to be—a third version, reaching necessarily back to 1944 and 1945. This is that the American concern with Russia came not too early but too late; that Stalin should have been confronted with precise and practical questions about the actual limits of his postwar sphere of interest, including the political status of at least some of the countries overrun by the Russian armies, sooner rather than later, in 1944 or early 1945, but certainly before the end of the Second World War in Europe.

Such an interpretation was mentioned by this author in some of his books. Much more important is that such a desideratum was advanced by personages such as Churchill and George Kennan. The former's views were mentioned in this chapter earlier; but I must turn, briefly, to Kennan, whose "X" article in 1947 laid down the principles of "containment," often designated as the substance of the architecture of American policy during the Cold War. Six years earlier, in 1941, Kennan was an officer in the American embassy in Berlin. After the German invasion of the Soviet Union he wrote a private letter to his friend Loy Henderson in Washington, the gist of which was: "Never—neither then nor at any later date—did I consider the Soviet Union a fit ally or associate, actual or potential, for [the United States]." At the same time he thought that the Russians should be given the material and military support they needed. One may question whether such a combination of military assistance with political aloofness could have been practical or reasonable at all. But one should not question the reasonableness and the foresight of Kennan's views when he was posted to Russia in 1944, especially after the Allies' invasion of Western Europe. Now the problem was "what would be the political outcome of further advances of the Red Army into the remainder of Europe."[16] It took another year before Kennan's voice was beginning to be heard—first by his ambassador Harriman; then in February 1946 Kennan wrote his now famous Long Telegram; then he was called back to Washington, where he became the director of a Foreign Policy Planning Staff; then in July 1947 came his "X" article with the celebrated word *Containment*. This article made him famous, yet its essence was perhaps a restatement of what has become obvious: the Russians have Eastern Europe now, and we must let them and the world know that they cannot go farther. It sometimes happens that an author is best known for a piece of writing that he himself does not see as his best. But here we must go a little beyond that. Soon after 1947, Kennan (as well as Churchill) turned against those who thought and spoke as if Stalin's and Russia's ambitions were endless and the division of Europe nonnegotiable and unchangeable. Their arguments were dismissed as illusory—by many of the same men who in 1945 had thought and said that to Churchill's and to Kennan's warnings about Russia attention must not be paid.

That is another story. So let me return to the main question, which perhaps ought to be rephrased: for behind (and within) the question of whether the Cold War was inevitable there is another question: was Stalin insatiable? Yes and no. So far as his rule over his own people and over his acquired domains went, yes; but so far as the rest of the world, and particularly Western Europe, went, probably no. There is no evidence that, either in 1945 or after, he aimed or even wished to have the Red Army march farther into Europe, or to establish Communist regimes in Western Europe, or even in Western Germany. This was not so only because he was statesman enough to be cautious. It was so, too, because of his knowledge of the weakness of international Communism. That was the reason of the "iron curtain," the increasingly rigid separation of Eastern Europe from the West. Had he agreed to (as some in the State Department hoped as late as in 1946) an interpretation of the Yalta Declaration of Liberated Europe and of his sphere of interest to allow the presence of governments in Eastern Europe that would be categorically and necessarily pro-Russian but not necessarily Communist,[17] there might not have been much of a, or any, Cold War. We may even speculate that if something like that had occurred, Russia could have been a recipient of American generosity, perhaps even of a super–Marshall Plan. But could Stalin have agreed to something like that?[18] No, he was not that kind of a man. No, but not because of his Marxist or Communist or ideological extremism, as so many still believe and say and write. He knew that sooner or later a non-Communist Poland or Czechoslovakia or Hungary, no matter how carefully their governments stayed and kept within their categorical requirements of a pro-Russian policy, would be gradually growing closer to the West, connected by a thousand small threads, some more important than others. It was safer, and to him better, to impose on these people rulers who were totally subservient to and dependent on Russia—and to close them off from the rest of Western Europe, no matter how Americans and others might protest.

That was how the Cold War began. The Russians swallowed up Eastern Europe; then it went on for forty years, during which they had serious instances of digesting some of it (as Churchill had foretold);[19] and it ended with their disgorging just about all of it. But one of the results of the Cold War was the American national and popular obsession with the evils of Communism that became the principal element in American politics with long-lasting effects. What may belong here is at least a suggestion that the Cold War between America and Russia might also have been—at least in one important way—due to a reciprocal misunderstanding. Americans believed, and feared, that, having established Communism in Eastern Europe, Stalin was now ready to promote and wherever possible impose Communism in Western Europe, which was not really the case. Stalin, who knew and understood the weak appeal of Communism beyond the Soviet Union, and who was anxious about America's overwhelming power in and after 1945, thought that the Americans were becoming ready to challenge and upset his rule over Eastern Europe, which also was not the case. The odd thing is that in Europe the turning point of the Cold War came in 1956, at the time of the Hungarian Revolution, which stunned and shocked the Russian leadership; but it also gave them a recognition of relief: the Americans were not ready or willing to really challenge or even attempt to alter the division of Europe. That this turning point of American-Russian relations in Europe coincided with a peak of—understandably, because of the brutal Russian suppression of Hungary—American popular hostility for Communism and Russia is, again, another instance of the irony of history (or, perhaps, of the melancholy history of what goes under the imprecise name of "public opinion"). After 1956 in Europe the enmity of the two Superpowers was gradually winding down, until the political division of Europe and of Germany ended with the withdrawal of the Russian empire in 1989. And the end of the Cold War meant also the end of an entire historical century, of the twentieth, dominated by the effects and the results of two world wars.

Allow me to append a coda to these considerations.

History does not repeat itself: but there was a geographic similarity to the once strategy of the British and thereafter of the American empires. During four centuries England went to war when a single state threatened to rule Europe, and particularly Western European countries, across the English Channel. In the First and the Second World Wars and the Cold War, across the Atlantic, American statesmanship saw the keeping of Britain and of Western Europe safe from German and then from the prospect of Russian domination as prime and essential American interests. During and after the Second World War, this convergence of American and British and Western European interests reached their peak.

More than strategic considerations were involved here. For more than a century and a half after 1776, America moved westward, away from Europe. This was not only a geographic and demographic and strategic direction. It corresponded to the American national and popular belief of the New World's destiny being the opposite of the Old's: *Novus Ordo Seclorum*. In 1917 came a great change: for the first time a large American army crossed the Atlantic from west to east to help decide a great European war. Soon after that the majority of the American people repudiated that expedition. Yet that repudiation was not entire. During the 1920s the commercial, the intellectual, the cultural ties between the United States and Europe were not diminishing: they were extending. Then came the Second World War, and the apparent ending of American isolationism.

In December 1945, Professor Carlton Hayes, a great American scholar and eminent historian of modern Europe, gave a remarkable presidential address at the convention of the American Historical Association. He said that Frederick Jackson Turner's famous frontier thesis, according to which the history and the destiny and the very essence of the American people were determined by a constant and uninterrupted movement westward, thus away from the East Coast, the Atlantic, and Europe, was mistaken. The Second World War itself demonstrated how the destinies—indeed, the civilizations and the cultures—of the United States and Western Europe were complementary, because they belonged together. That complementarity seemed evident during the Second World War and at least during the first phase of the Cold War, when not only strategists and statesmen but many cultured and liberally educated Americans welcomed the end of a protracted isolationism, accepting an American peacetime commitment to, and an American presence and a military and political connection with, Western Europe.

Rightly so . . . but that was nearly sixty years ago. Now there are, lo and behold, entire Eastern European states within NATO, and there is an American military presence in such formerly unimaginable places as Romania, Macedonia, Afghanistan. At the same time . . . one may ask whether America and Europe are not growing apart? What is not questionable is that the weight of the United States has been shifting westward and southward; and so has the composition of its population—at the beginning of a new age, well after anything like the Second World War.

Six

The Vital Center Did Not Hold

Providence allowed Arthur Schlesinger a long life, with an almost perfect ending. He had written and published the first volume of his autobiography after his eighty-third birthday. Six years later, in 2006, he showed to his literary agent and to his sons the six thousand pages of his diaries that he kept from 1952 to 2000. They chose to publish an abridged volume, consisting of about one-sixth of these pages, to be presented on the festive date of his ninetieth birthday in October 2007. He died while dining in a good New York restaurant—an appropriate setting, since Schlesinger had had a healthy appetite for fine food and drink—seven months before that planned event. Departing thus from life: an almost perfect conclusion to the career of this political historian and literary man.

Diaries or private journals cannot, by their very nature, be perfect, because of the circumstances and the time in which they are written. A classic example is the diaries of Evelyn Waugh, which are inferior to his letters, because (as we were told by his biographers) he wrote sparkling, intimate letters each morning, and he wrote his diaries in the evening, when he was often drunk and tired. Diaries and journals may be interesting because of their double function: they tell us some things about the people and the times of their confection and, even more, about the private life and thinking of their writers. These two elements are seldom balanced. Worth considering is the purpose of the diarist. Did he write mainly to clear his own mind? Or was the principal purpose of his diaries to have a record for the future, or to enhance his posthumous reputation? It is not easy to distinguish these purposes. Often the most revealing diaries are those that were not meant for publication.

We ought not criticize Schlesinger's sons for their dutifulness and effort to put his journals together: after all, their father had told them to do just that. But the worth of these journals is another matter. Their father wrote easily. From their introduction: "A superior diarist with a masterful style. His journals were full of rich, witty and revelatory observations about the famous events and larger-than-life personalities in American life for nearly five decades." Filial respect is always commendable. But their father was not a superior diarist.

In 1952, when these journals begin, Arthur Schlesinger was thirty-four years old, a rather well-known historian, and already something of a public figure. Yet there is a considerable immaturity in these early diaries, though they do get a little more interesting as his career proceeds. Moreover, there is something odd in the composition—that is, in the selections printed in this otherwise very large (more than nine hundred pages) volume. There is only one entry for the year 1953; only two entries for the year 1954; and there are no entries for two full years, 1958 and 1999. It appears that Schlesinger wrote his journals intermittently—almost as if they were second thoughts, marginal efforts about events and people he considered worth recording. Besides, six hundred pages are not that many for a diary supposedly kept for half a century. In his entries from the 1950s, for example, when Schlesinger was more and more involved in politics and elections, there is almost nothing about the national crisis produced by Joseph McCarthy in 1953 and 1954. In 1960, when Schlesinger became a special adviser to John Kennedy, there is nothing about the U-2 crisis, about Kennedy meeting with Khrushchev in Vienna, about the erection of the Berlin Wall. There is plenty in the 1979 and 1980 journals about the odd coincidence of Richard Nixon's having bought a house on East 64th Street in New York immediately adjoining the Schlesingers': amusing as some of these details are, revelatory they are not.

A celebrity is someone who is famous for being well known—a witticism true enough to have become a cliché. Was Arthur M. Schlesinger Jr. a celebrity? Yes and no. Even if he did not much wish to become one, he *was* well known. That was both a condition and a circumstance that he relished, with gusto, and he had an undiscriminating appetite for the company of celebrities of all kinds. About that there are hundreds of entries in these journals. In July 1960 his diary entry about the Democratic National Convention (during which he was very busy) includes a long account of a party in which he finds it essential to record those present "from Max Lerner to Gina Lollobrigida" as well as his serious conversations with Jack Lemmon (about Billy Wilder), Charlton Heston, Shelley Winters, and others. On another occasion Marilyn Monroe "receded into her own glittering mist"—whatever that means. I suggested earlier that Schlesinger's journals improve as he gets older, but about these people and their parties there is no improvement. Thirty-two years later, in 1992: "Much talk about Woody Allen, Mia Farrow and their break-up . . . they seemed rather adorable together." Adorable? In 2000: "We saw the debate at Norman Mailer's." Etcetera, etcetera. A question arises in my mind: Was Schlesinger a namedropper? Again: yes and no. He liked to impress people by telling them how many famous people he knew. Yet as he wrote his diaries he must have felt compelled to record those names mainly to please himself. With the exception of a rare glimpse of doubt—"The gossip of the idle rich is exceedingly boring"—there is not much self-inspection in these diaries. Journals are often superficial—a condition that is unavoidable, constrained as diaries are by their writers' situation in the present. Nonetheless, when writers skate above or stop at inevitable moments of their lives, they are aware of what is below. But Schlesinger's entries lack such depth. They are often both superficial and shallow.

In the *Journals*, Schlesinger reveals himself to be vain. No matter: most of us are. His ambitions were both social and political. That, too, is not unusual. What is interesting, and telling, is that his ambitions compromised—indeed, they often obscured—his judgment. Even that is not unusual: it is the occupational disease of opportunists. But whereas the successful opportunist succeeds in deceiving others, Arthur Schlesinger often deceived himself. There are many evidences of this throughout his journals. He was a feverish fan of Adlai Stevenson throughout the 1950s (and even after), but once John Kennedy took Schlesinger as one of his advisers, Schlesinger did not just change allegiances; he ran headlong into the Kennedy corral. He convinced himself that switching to Kennedy was no different from supporting Stevenson. Did it not occur to him that this was akin to opportunism? Nothing in his journals suggests this. He became close to the Kennedys, often to the extent of fawning over them, though not quite as close as he presents himself in these journals (and later in entire big books), and perhaps not as close as he himself thought. He had no compunction about transferring liege lordship from Jack to Bobby Kennedy; indeed, he hoped to be a prime Kennedy satellite as late as 1980, wishing for Edward Kennedy to become a presidential candidate. Jack and Bob and Ted were three very different brothers. Schlesinger remained the same.

Jack had put him in the East and not the West Wing of the White House. On occasion there is an acknowledgment that he was not at all at the center of events. There is only one entry in these journals of the thirteen days from October 16 to 28, 1962, when the Cuban crisis was unfolding: "My connection with all this was—and remained—peripheral." A rare admission. On the day John Kennedy is shot: "I heard the terrible news as I was sipping cocktails with Kay Graham, Ken Galbraith and the editors of *Newsweek*."

Joseph Lelyveld wrote in the *New York Review of Books* that Schlesinger's "*Journals* deserve to be welcomed as an unexpected gift. . . . [They] cohere surprisingly well as a book about the passing political spectacle over half a century by a fugitive scholar." This is too much. Schlesinger was a political historian but even when he was close to important events he was easily capable of illusions. In 1959, about Kennedy: "And he obviously regards Stevenson as inevitable for Secretary of State." Obviously? No. Not at all. One year later: "Under Truman the essence of the Democratic appeal was to promise benefits;

under Kennedy it is to demand sacrifices; what conclusive evidence of the Stevensonian triumph! Kennedy is the heir and executor of the Stevensonian revolution—whether either Jack or Adlai realize this fact." Conclusive evidence? Fact? A fatuous example of self-deception this is. In 1962 about Nixon's book *Six Crises*: "I do not see how his political career can survive this book." Well, survive it did, all the way to two Nixon presidencies. In the same year, Schlesinger is worried "about the developing new restraints on the presidential power." The very opposite was happening then, and ever since.

Whatever the value of these journals, it is not so much in what they reveal about their writer but in what he occasionally records of the words and the behavior of others—and sometimes contrary to his earlier and standard judgments of them. Notice what he writes about his idol Adlai Stevenson, two days after John Kennedy's assassination: "Stevenson came in, smiling and chipper, as if nothing at all had happened." About another idol, John Kenneth Galbraith (in my opinion a champion opportunist, confirmed by this): on the day after the assassination, "a telephone call from Ken reported that he had seen Johnson, and that Johnson had asked him to work with Sorensen on the message. Ken seemed in high spirits." On pages 335 and 336, Schlesinger records what Averell Harriman said about Stalin and Roosevelt, on the subject of the former's awe of the latter: a precious nugget of information, alas, of use only to serious historians of the Second World War and the origins of the Cold War. From 1959 to 1962 there are four short snippets recording John Kennedy's disdain for Eisenhower; in 1983 there is a page-and-a-half account of a lunch with George Plimpton, who talked to Schlesinger about Ernest Hemingway. Kennedy's few words are worth recounting; Plimpton's stories are not.

When Schlesinger was seventy-four, what he wrote when he was forty-two, in 1960, was still true: "I must say that I adore sitting around hotel rooms with politicians and newspapermen exchanging gossip over drinks." In 1992, "like an old firehorse, I respond to the ringing of the campaign bell." However, there are signs, here and there, of the maturing of his mind. There is one, surely unwitting, example of this. In 1959 a snooty Schlesinger is dismissive of Harry Truman, who tells him about a trip to France and his dislike of Picasso: "On Modern Art, [Truman] was, as usual, at his worst." Thirty-four years later, in 1993, a rueful admission, at the Gropius Museum in Berlin: "I suppose it reveals my philistinism . . . but Warhol, Barnett Newman, Roy Lichtenstein, Julian Schnabel, Richard Serra, etc. seem such transparent fakes and con men, and it is almost shaming to see American hype hung and captioned with such reverence abroad." In 1979, writing about his statuary monumental idol Franklin Roosevelt: "A fascinating figure—not probably a great man but certainly a great President." "Not probably a great man"? This is not what Arthur Schlesinger would have written—or thought—thirty or even twenty years before. And in 1986, *aetatis* sixty-eight: "I have no faith, none at all, in progress. I do not expect a better future." Thus wrote this former progressive and populist liberal.

Here I arrive at the main shortcoming of the *Journals*. A few reviewers have criticized Schlesinger (mildly) for having been too much of a social butterfly. But what these diaries reveal is something deeper and broader than those innumerable outcroppings of vanity. The trouble is their author's constricted historical and political vision; his failure to comprehend—indeed, even to recognize—what was happening to his nation during his lifetime.

In 1952, when his journals begin and when he was thirty-four, there were hardly any American political figures who would call themselves "conservative"—not Robert A. Taft, not even Joseph McCarthy. Eight years later, on one occasion, a president (Eisenhower) refers to himself as "conservative." Four years later, the Republican presidential nominee (Goldwater) announces that he is "a conservative." Another sixteen years later, Ronald Reagan, a self-declared conservative, is elected president by an overwhelming majority. By that time—1980—more Americans identify themselves as conservatives than as liberals. This was, and remains, a tectonic transformation, unprecedented in American history. Its meaning escapes Arthur Schlesinger entirely.

He was, as were so many of his liberal friends, hopelessly out of date. So are his editors. In their short Introduction to his *Journals*, they write: "It is not an exaggeration to say that his broad circle of friends—both men and women—virtually dominated the political, social, artistic and literary landscape of [his] era." Was this so? Schlesinger's circles of friends consisted, without exception, of Democrats and liberals. But have Democrats and liberals "virtually dominated" the American political landscape from 1952 to 2000? During the past forty years, in seven elections out of ten, the American people chose presidents who were Republicans and who called themselves conservatives. Only once or twice, as late as the Reagan era, Schlesinger jots down an admission in his diary about "the restricted circles in which I move." Or about Reagan's invasion of Grenada, or about the first President Bush's invasion of Panama, or then about the war against Iraq in 1991: "Nearly everyone one knows is against the war too. That shows the restricted circles in which I move since, according to the polls, 80 per cent of Americans favor the war." (Indeed, at least 68 percent were in favor of the invasions of Grenada and Panama, and in 2003, 75 percent were in favor of the second war against Iraq.)

In one of his later books, *The Cycles of American History* (1986), Schlesinger wrote that the political history of his country and of its people has progressed through great successive waves of more liberal and less liberal periods. The book was universally praised, but this scheme, or vision, is outdated and wrong. The liberal vs. conservative debate or dialogue took place in Europe and England rather than in America. There was no real conservative party, or movement, in the United States. There were some Americans during the nineteenth century whom we may see, by and large, as conservatives; but almost all of them refused to designate themselves as such.

Then, after about 1870, in Europe and in England too, the great debate between liberals and conservatives started to lose its meaning. Two new political forces began to appear and to replace them. One was nationalism, which was something different from an older kind of patriotism, and the other was socialism, which was no longer revolutionary but espoused the welfare state. During the twentieth century, and especially after World War II, these designations became applicable to the great American divisions and to the two main political parties in the United States: the Republicans being more nationalist than socialist, the Democrats more socialist than nationalist. Still, the adjectives we may affix to these parties do not much matter. What matters is the rapid decline of the appeal of liberalism, and the attraction and the force of a populist nationalism—the cult of the people and of the military power of the nation, the meaning of which Schlesinger cannot comprehend or perhaps even discern. In 1955, William F. Buckley Jr. launched his *National Review*, his "conservative"—

much more accurately, his nationalist—weekly on a shoestring. Forty years later it had more subscribers than *The Nation* and the *New Republic* together (and the worldview of the latter had begun to move in a neoconservative direction). As late as 1989, Schlesinger saw the collapse of the Soviet empire as the long overdue triumph of democracy against Communism. He failed to see that the dissolution of the Soviet empire as well as the popularity *of*, say, Ronald Reagan were due not to the appeal of liberal democracy but to the appeal of nationalism. Until the last pages of his journals and, presumably, till the very end of his life, Schlesinger kept writing and thinking about Democrats and Republicans, liberals versus anti-liberals.

His early book *The Age of Jackson*, published in 1945, was a bestseller, and it made Arthur Schlesinger Jr. famous. That his then hero Andrew Jackson had nothing in common with his later heroes, such as Stevenson or Kennedy (though Jackson had a little more in common with another Southerner, Lyndon Johnson, whom Schlesinger came to loathe), is worth noting, but that is not my argument now. The main problem is that Schlesinger's view of history was flawed. And why? Because of his view of human nature—and does not any understanding of history rest on some understanding of human nature? In *The Age of Jackson*, the young Arthur Schlesinger Jr., quoting Pascal, wrote this sentence: "Man is neither angel nor brute"—a safe, liberal, gray, centrist view of human nature. To the contrary: man is both angel and brute.

This is something that Schlesinger, whose next book after *The Age of Jackson* bore the title *The Vital Center*, never understood—or perhaps never even thought about. He was a decent man. He had a pleasant career. But his journals are those of a very shortsighted historian.

Seven

A Tocqueville Tide

More than two hundred years after Tocqueville's birth (1805), his international reputation is greater than ever. Proof of this is the increasing number of books and articles about him. Of course, their value varies. There is, however, a salutary development. We live at a time when, amid innumerable evidences of cultural and civilizational decay, the art of biography flourishes. Regarding Tocqueville we are beneficiaries of that. We are now, more than before, able to read and know much about Tocqueville the man. It was not until 1984 that the first serious and scholarly biography of Tocqueville was published, written by André Jardin, a Tocqueville scholar and one of the principal editors of Tocqueville's *Oeuvres Complètes.* Now we have two other very substantial ones, whose contents do more than complement Jardin's. Their emphasis may be seen in their subtitles: Hugh

Brogan, *Alexis de Tocqueville: A Life* (2006); Jean-Louis Benoît, *Tocqueville: Un destin paradoxal* (2005).

Hugh Brogan's is a monumental achievement. It is a model of biography and of honest scholarship. He does not fail to give credit to those who have written about this or that event in Tocqueville's life, no matter how marginal. We may regret that he could not have read Benoît's (and Mancini's—see below) works before completing his own, but that circumstance does not reduce his merits. There is his writing: his very English biographical style is superb. Add to this his excellent knowledge of French, including his understanding of those subtle nuances of differences between English and French words which exist despite their common origins and dictionary equivalences (*honnête homme*, referring to a lowly cook: "one of us"); or consider Brogan's discussion of *moeurs*—a very important term and theme for Tocqueville—adding in a learned footnote: "It is a difficult expression to render in English, comprising as it does morals, manners, and customs." Then there is his deep and wide knowledge of French political and social history in the nineteenth century. And not only French history. Example: in 1835 in England, Tocqueville met the then young Camille Cavour, who described Tocqueville at some length; and these valuable two paragraphs in Brogan's book are not taken from Tocqueville's papers but from Cavour's journals. (Two other random examples of the stunning extent of what Brogan knows: a Tocqueville cousin who was probably the imaginary villain of the "Scarlet Pimpernel" stories; that in 1855 the Tocquevilles lived on a small street in Paris where Gertrude Stein was to live sixty years later.)

One of Brogan's most important contributions is his extensive and sympathetic account of Tocqueville's wife, about whom, until recently, readers knew little or nothing. We now have a portrait of Madame de Tocqueville, the former Marie Mottley, which promises to remain enduring. She was a middle-class Englishwoman, six years older than her husband. Their marriage was a *mésalliance*, not favored by her husband's family. But now we know (and in this their lately published correspondence in the *Oeuvres Complètes* was a help) that the marriage was, unlike many arranged aristocratic marriages, a success. That condition was doubted or dismissed by the few Frenchmen who wrote about Tocqueville and his marriage earlier. It also appears that Marie was not at all unattractive, unintellectual, stolid, quarrelsome, or a heavy handicap on Tocqueville's life and mind. Brogan writes that Tocqueville "needed women for much more than sex; or perhaps it would be more accurate to say that for him sex could comprehend much more than eager physical pleasure. He wanted mothering . . . he needed tenderness and reassurance. He also needed forgiveness and patience; he was well aware of his faults. He needed companionship." Brogan says that Tocqueville's decision to visit the United States was "by most measures . . . the most important decision of his life." Yet Tocqueville said, and not once, that it was his marrying Marie. In any event Brogan's summary of his choice is just and generous. "In spite of all . . . Tocqueville had triumphed and acted in accordance with his consistent beliefs. Nothing he ever did was more democratic, modern, or honourable."

We shall see that Brogan's judgment of *Democracy in America* (henceforth *DA*) is mixed. He has few reservations about the quality of the *Souvenirs*; and almost none about *L'Ancien Régime* (henceforth *AR*), whose virtues he sees as a historian should. Like the excellent Robert Gannett, Brogan follows how that "masterpiece" was made. The development of Tocqueville's work in the archives "would do credit to a student nowadays following one of those formidable French doctoral theses." "Tocqueville's research into the archives of the old order and the interpretations which he put upon his results really seem to have been unprecedented." Moreover, Tocqueville "took endless pains with his style, and erected a monument of French literature." Earlier: "Not for Tocqueville any attempt at a sham-objective 'scientific' prose." Brogan's conclusion: "Great historians do not just record or explain the past; they awaken it, and their readers. . . . Tocqueville was equal to that challenge, as can also be demonstrated by comparing his book with almost any recent study of merit on the same subject." Brogan is very good, too, about the sometimes debated question of Tocqueville's last days in Cannes. His conclusion is terse and just: "The surprise, perhaps, is that he left the Church rather than that he returned to it."

I must now move to my few disagreements with this truly magisterial biography. Here and there Brogan sounds a tad patronizing. In his otherwise superb *Souvenirs*, Tocqueville, on occasion, "sneers." "Much of *Democracy in America* is written with the . . . purpose [of] self-justification." In the letters of Tocqueville and Beaumont from America, there is "a desperate attempt to make some sort of sense of their impressions; they filled their letters with rash generalizations based on little evidence and no experience (a trait which Tocqueville was never entirely to throw off)." Brogan is critical of Tocqueville and Beaumont for not having met and listened to anyone in the United States save for distinguished people with whom "they felt most at home . . . they thus forfeited one of the advantages of foreign travel." This is—at least partly—contradicted by an important passage from Tocqueville's notebooks that Brogan cites: "One thing is incontrovertibly demonstrated in America which I doubted until now: it is that the middle classes can govern a State." Brogan does not mention a very important condition: how and why Tocqueville in *DA* refers throughout to the American people as "Anglo-Americans."

The one—and only—substantial disagreement I have with Brogan (who, I should add, honored me by allowing me to read his entire manuscript, and who praised a long-ago printed contribution of mine) involves his judgment of the second volume of *DA*. I (and in this sense I am not alone) regard the second volume of *DA* as even more important than the first; Brogan does not. "It is even half true that he had nothing to say which he had not already put into the 1835 *Democratie*; the 1840 *Democratie*, in a sense, is simply a vast elaboration." Not "even half true," I venture to think. Nor is it true that while liberty "was the guiding star of his life . . . in 1840 he seems to have understood it even less than he did equality. He never seriously asks what it might mean to anyone except people like himself." I also regret that Brogan did not mention that stunningly profound and prescient short chapter in *DA II* about how history may be written in democratic ages. And about Tocqueville's no less profound and prophetic chapter "Why Revolutions Will Become Rare," Brogan writes: "that chapter seems to be the work of an author who is not quite convinced by his own arguments." But how convincing that chapter still is!

One of the merits of Brogan's biography is his extensive treatment of Tocqueville's political career. Whether in 1837, Tocqueville, standing for election, "was little more than a carpet-bag candidate" may be arguable. And the claim that "at no point in 1848 did Tocqueville display the slightest fellow-feeling for the workers in their distress, and consequently had no gleam of understanding them" is not quite fair; nor is Brogan's assertion that Tocqueville "was not even exceptional in

expressing his fear in ideological terms as if he were resolved to demonstrate the accuracy of the Marxian tenet that ideas are determined by material circumstances, and have no other validity." Though a hypothesis, this goes to the very contrary of Tocqueville's political thinking, which is that ideas and their movements are often anterior and sometimes even more decisive than are material conditions. In another remarkable and perceptive footnote, Brogan writes that there is only one mention of Tocqueville "so far as I know, in all the works of Marx"—to which we may add that, conversely, there is no evidence (and why should there be?) that Tocqueville knew anything of Marx at all. One last, very minor, correction of the otherwise so often splendid prose of this British and Protestant writer: it is not quite accurate to say that, after his crisis of belief in his early youth, Tocqueville "abandoned Catholicism." But otherwise Brogan's account of that crisis is very good.

Yet despite all his criticism of *DA II*, Brogan—to his great credit—writes: "In the end Tocqueville rose above all difficulties and inconsistencies and composed the last page of the book, one of the noblest things he ever wrote. It is Tocqueville at his best, both as a man and a thinker. It must be quoted in full." There follows a great passage.[1] "Thus, after years of painful thought, Tocqueville expressed the creed he meant to live by—and that indeed he lived by, until his death."

Tocqueville is always clear. But researchers of his work have had and still have particular problems to face. There is his difficult handwriting. There is the enormous mass of his papers. He was a compulsive writer, and at least some of his most interesting and inspiring statements may be found in his many thousands of private letters. And there is yet another problem, that of terminology. Brogan asks the question: What did Tocqueville mean by "the loss of our aristocracy"? Brogan's father, Sir Denis Brogan (to whom—"My Father—Teacher—Inspiration"—his son's *Tocqueville* is lovingly dedicated), wrote many years ago a trenchant sentence in his brilliant introduction to the *Memoirs of Saint Simon*: "As Tocqueville pointed out," by the time of Louis XIV "France no longer had an aristocracy, only *noblesse*." But in 1856, writing *AR*, did Tocqueville equate aristocracy with *noblesse*? I do not think so. He believed (in this respect England was a sort of example to him) that *some* kind of aristocracy remains necessary to counterbalance a degeneration of democracy into demagogic populism. What remains arguable is whether Tocqueville, who was of course a nobleman by birth, had a nostalgia for an aristocratic order that compromised his vision of democracy. I do not think so, but at times Brogan does.

Jean-Louise Benoît's *Tocqueville* is a very valuable biography, worthy to be a companion of Brogan's. The latter's style and thinking is very English; Benoît's very French. These are respective and complementary virtues. Benoît's great merit is his detailed acquaintance with Tocqueville's papers; added to that, he is *sur place*. Living close to the château and hamlet of Tocqueville, he is intimately acquainted with the history and details of Tocqueville's family.

There is much to be learned from his detailed knowledge. Many of his footnotes furnish significant information. The Tocquevilles acquired their château from relatives as late as 1777; his notes from Alexis's father, Hervé, complement R. R. Palmer's *The Two Tocquevilles: Father and Son* (1987)—though there is no evidence that Benoît knows this work; an important letter was wrongly attributed in volume 13 of the *Oeuvres Complètes*; a very long and detailed footnote tells us much about the still somewhat obscure question of how and when Tocqueville and Marie Mottley first met; we learn that Alexis's first love affair (with Rosalie Malye) began when he was only sixteen, that Alexis became Marie's lover in late 1828 (both Rosalie and Marie were older than Tocqueville), that Alexis was unhappy when his widowed father married his mistress, that Tocqueville's faithful Dr. Andral was Royer-Collard's son-in-law; etc. Benoît gives us detailed demographic and electoral statistics about Tocqueville's *département*, La Manche, including an analysis of who supported him among the local legitimists and who did not. In 1830 Tocqueville was required to take an oath of loyalty to the new regime of the bourgeois monarchy; his inclination was to refuse, but then his father, his brothers, and Beaumont convinced him not to do that. In a footnote Benoît writes: "Unfortunately his biographers state the contrary." (Not so Brogan, whose treatment of Tocqueville's then profound dilemma is detailed and excellent.) Benoît tells us that Tocqueville's original title for *DA II* was *L'influence de l'égalité sur les idées et les sentiments des hommes*, which his new publisher, Gosselin, wisely told him to discard. While Brogan, as we have seen, is critical of *DA II*, Benoît recognizes its enduring importance. (Brogan could hardly have read Benoît: completion of their works occurred almost at the same time.)

Benoît is right that a book about Tocqueville's foreign ministership in 1849—in my opinion, long overdue—is yet to be written. Perhaps one shortcoming of his excellent work: Benoît's treatment of Tocqueville's life after 1849 may be too short and fast, not more than forty pages. Also, there are many footnotes in which Benoît, perhaps unnecessarily, refers to French politics in the twentieth century (surely unnecessary is his very first footnote paying homage to Hannah Arendt and George Steiner). But in addition to his trove of significant details, there is much that is valuable in Benoît's general judgments: “Public opinion knows very well how to lie to itself ”; Tocqueville was not a *maître penseur* but a *maître á penser.* Benoît is right in pointing out that even recent historians, “from Braudel to Furet, passing through Lefebvre,” failed to say anything interesting or important about *AR*. In a substantial subchapter about Tocqueville’s views on the military in democratic societies, Benoît is critical of Raymond Aron’s neglect of that subject.

A much smaller book, *Alexis de Tocqueville: Notes sur le Coran et autres texts sur les religions*, was published, introduced, and annotated by Benoît in 2007. It consists of entire texts of some of Tocqueville’s letters and notes on Islam, Hinduism, Christianity, and Catholicism. That Tocqueville was *essentiellement agnostique* but at the same time *spiritualiste* is debatable: such phrases depend on the variable, rather than the precise meaning, of such French words. That Tocqueville had an almost “visceral reticence” against the dogmas of the Immaculate Conception and of Original Sin is questionable: the Pascalian Tocqueville surely did not reject Original Sin. A long footnote amounts to a discussion—and a thoughtful rejection—of some recent articles about Tocqueville and Algeria, of which Tocqueville’s opinions considerably changed from the 1830s into the early 1840s.

Besides their other merits, the previously discussed three books fill many small gaps in our knowledge of Tocqueville. Matthew Mancini’s *Alexis de Tocqueville and American Intellectuals: From His Times to Ours* (2006) fills a very large one, whence it deserves considerable attention. The accepted opinion is that Tocqueville’s influence and reputation quickly waned after his death, reappearing only about 1950. In 1993 Françcoise Mélonio—the principal Tocqueville expert of our times—in his *Tocqueville et les Français* carefully examined and corrected the evidences of this in France. That Tocqueville's reputation was in relative eclipse in his own country until about 1950 is largely true, but not in the United States. That is the essence of Mancini's very important work. It is a pity that neither Brogan nor Benoît could peruse it before completing their biographies.

Mancini offers a thoughtful distinction between the reputation and the reception of a thinker and his work. "A thinker's reputation is a cultural artifact . . . eminently suitable to analysis. . . . Reception is a historical *process*, reputation *a product*." He describes in detail the often overlooked relationship of Tocqueville to Francis Lieber, who may have been for a long time Tocqueville's principal exegete in the United States. But of course Lieber was not alone: there were Charles Eliot Norton, in whose opinion Tocqueville's reputation in the 1860s was waxing, not waning; Francis Bowen, for a long time Tocqueville's best translator into English; George W. Curtis; E. L. Godkin, founder of the *Nation*—all of them American interpreters of *AR*, the last one the first to relate Tocqueville to Edmund Burke. Mancini provides more than ample evidence for his assertion that Tocqueville's reputation and influence in the United States remained considerable and even constant after 1870. The last chapters of his book are thoughtful essays about Tocqueville's influence in the United States throughout most of the twentieth century. Their titles are telling: "An Enduring Sage"; "A Cottage Industry"; "Lumpers and Splitters."

The Cambridge Companion to Tocqueville (2006), edited by Cheryl B. Welch, is uneven. The introduction by its editor is wanting. She is unaware of Mancini: "The full story of Tocqueville's reception in the United States has not yet been told." In a chronology, the summary of 1859 offers the following: "Marie convinced her husband to confess and receive Holy Communion, but it is not known whether he recovers his faith." This is wrong, as is this badly hobbling passage: "Tocqueville aspired to create a democratic language with which to negotiate the nineteenth-century transition to democracy. Although he failed in that aim, the persona he created has paradoxically succeeded in becoming a powerful voice in subsequent democratic discussions, and not only in Europe." Among the fourteen essays, Seymour Drescher's "Tocqueville's Comparative Perspectives," James T. Schleifer's "Tocqueville's *Democracy in America* Reconsidered," Robert T. Gannett's "The Shifting Puzzles of Tocqueville's *The Old Regime and the Revolution*," and Laurence Guellec's "The Writer *Engagé*: Tocqueville and Political Rhetoric" are very good. Joshua Mitchell's "Tocqueville on Democratic Religious Experience" is interesting but, oddly, contains little about Tocqueville. Jon Elster's "Tocqueville on 1789: Preconditions, Precipitants, and Triggers" (a strange colonic subtitle) is badly wanting: "*Democracy in America*, while full of striking insights of lasting value, is badly structured and often incoherent." Yes? "Given Louis XVI's character, the Revolution was a certainty." No. Harvey C. Mansfield Jr. and Delba Winthrop in "Tocqueville's New Political Science": "The degree of soul [?] necessary to liberalism, according to Tocqueville, is not perfection but pride." This about a man who said that while the main vice of aristocracies was pride, that of democracies is envy. Arthur Goldhammer's "Translating Tocqueville: The Constraints of Classicism" is a scholarly treatise by a master.

Eight

The World Around Me: My Adopted Country

The history of every country is unique. But the problems of American history are special, too, because of the structure of its democratic society—and that involves the very structure of its events. The history of a democracy is more difficult to write—properly—than the history of an aristocratic or semiaristocratic nation, since it must include more than the history of a governing class and of a state; it must involve the history of a majority of a people. But who *are* the people? What did they say? When and how did they speak? Where and what are the evidences of that? Is it not, rather, that these are people who spoke and chose and acted in the name of the people? If so, we are already one step removed from "reality." Yes, there is a vast multiplicity of records of what some people—notice: "*some* people," not "*the* people"—said and chose and did. But how did the consequent "facts," or events, come about? How did they happen; or, rather, how were they *made* to happen? The accumulation of opinions is what counts, not the accumulation of capital. But the persistent prediction of opinions may create public opinions (just as the prediction of profits leads to a rise in the price of shares). These matters are not simple.

American history is not simple. I am a historian who saw some of this from the very beginning of his life in the United States, in his adopted country. I wrote about these things on occasion. I think that I could still write a little book about the peculiar problems of the approaches, of the perspectives, of the methods, of the sources of American history, of its epistemology, of its hermeneutics. Now, in addition to its democratic complications, these matters have become ever more manageable and confusing and obscured by the burgeoning of technology and secrecy.[1] Also, popularity no longer merely *depends* on publicity; it has become *inseparable* from it. The complications now involve the liquefaction of the once categorical distinction between primary and secondary sources, because of the liquefaction of personal records, of what remains authentic and what is no longer so. There are enormous dark clouds massing above the blazing artificial lights of the people's stadia: obscureness unrecognized, unseen, unfelt by millions beneath, within the "show."

Now enough of this. I must limit myself to describing some things I saw and remember. Except for one last remark, or caveat: many things that I saw were not what many others saw. What happened was what people thought happened. I thought too that they happened: but sometimes I also thought that what happened meant something else. Usually beneath the surface: but then democratic surfaces are big and thick. Sometimes I was wrong.

Some time in the 1960s the behavior of many Americans changed. "Behavior" is not only superficial or external. When behavior changes, thinking changes too. There are few people in whose lives behavior and thinking are so interlaced, so dependent on each other, as in the United States, where images often not only clothe but absorb essence, where for many people to seem is as important as to be. (Two examples: In no other country does the description of a person in a newspaper report or even in a serious magazine article begin with a detailed description of his clothes. Or consider how the word, or observation, of "body language" is very American, appearing first in the 1960s: a foul-smelling phrase, is it not?)

There was the duality of the sixties. During that decade all kinds of public campaigns and legal reforms were, or at least pretended to be, concerned with the extension and the protection of the rights of individual privacy. Yet it was in the 1960s that so much of the presence and even the desire of personal privacy melted away. One evidence of that was the final disappearance of "society," its substitution being the cult of celebrity.

The bourgeois, the urban, period in the history of the United States lasted approximately from 1880 to 1950. This is a very large country, and there were vast exceptions, portions untouched by it, but so it was. America and Europe (and England) grew closer. America entered two world wars to help Britain, and Western Europe. After 1880 American cities grew larger than London, Paris, Berlin. The New World was no longer the antithesis of the opposite of the Old. It became the repository of its civilization, culture, arts. It was spared the catastrophes that befell Europe in the two world wars. Its institutions represented many of the values and the standards of a constitutional and liberal order. There was an American upper class whose power and ambitions were limited, but whose prestige was extant and attractive. But the convictions of their members were regrettably superficial, and their self-confidence remarkably weak. During the 1960s, they dissolved and disappeared, fast.[2] The behavior of their offspring changed instantly, together with what and how they thought.

Suburbanization, female emancipation,[3] civil rights for blacks, a loud cult of youth, television, a raucous sexual "revolution," a rise of divorces, of abortions, etc., etc.—of course they had forerunners, symptoms here and there evident in the fifties, and then much of these continued in the seventies and later: but my argument is that the sixties had two, at first sight contradictory, characteristics. Their happenings were ephemeral: but their effects were enduring. When in 1969 nearly half a million young Americans streamed to and crowded into a "festival" near Woodstock, New York, slews of disquisitions and articles declared this, breathlessly, as a revolution without precedent, with tremendous unforeseeable social and political consequences. In reality it resulted in nothing. What endured after the sixties were the mutations of behavior, ranging from clothes to habits, of manners as much as of morals. I am not writing this out of nostalgia for the America of the 1940s or 1950s: for the germinating symptoms of these changes had been already there. Then, in the 1960s, the bourgeois and urban and urbane chapter in the history of the United States of America came to its very end.[4]

As in so many instances this was (and still is) obscured by the falseness of the words categorizing it—with the result of problems wrongly stated. The enduring changes involved not "culture" but civilization. *Civilization* is a word that appears in English only in 1601, with its definition: "an emergence from barbarism."[5] The intellectualization of the word *culture*, mostly of German origin, came much later. The elevation of its prestige over *civilization* has caused enormous harm, especially in the history of Germany.[6] When civilization is strong and widespread enough, "culture" will appear and take care of itself.

The institutionalization of rights of women, of blacks, of homosexuals, for abortion, for semipornography, for free speech[7] and behavior, etc., looked and still look as extensions of liberalism, more juddering jolts toward a freer, more democratic, more liberal world. In reality, liberalism was dying. Ten years after the 1960s, it was just about dead. It belonged to the past; it had nothing more to achieve; it was exhausted. Its tasks had been done. It had emancipated hundreds of millions worldwide. I write *emancipated* rather than *freed*, because it is more difficult to be free than not to be free: but that is a perennial human predicament. In the United States the demise of Liberalism is clear and present in the history of words. In 1950 there was not one American public or political or academic or intellectual figure who declared himself *a* "conservative." By 1980 more Americans declared themselves "conservatives" than "liberals." They, including most professed American Christians, chose Ronald Reagan, a divorced movie actor, for their hero, for their president. This was a tectonic change in the political history of the United States that had no precedent. But the manners and morals of most American "conservatives" hardly differed from those of most other Americans, including "liberals."[8]

More than one hundred years ago, in Europe as well as in America, Public Opinion became absorbed by popular sentiment. Those who were interested in it, who attempted to identify it, ascertain it, measure it, continued to call it Public Opinion: another misuse of words. The same thing happened with the confusion of patriotism (old and traditional) with nationalism (new and democratic). I wrote about this elsewhere and I am loath to repeat myself. It may be enough to say that patriotism is defensive, while nationalism is aggressive; that patriotism means the love of a country, while nationalism is the cult of a people (and of the power of their state). Again we face the confusion of language: what Americans call a superpatriot is, in reality, a supernationalist. Throughout American history there have been many nationalist presidents; but few of them like Ronald Reagan, unabashedly so.

Then came the end of the Cold War, an immediate consequence of the implosion of the Soviet Union's empire with which Ronald Reagan (contrary to popular and "conservative" beliefs) had little to do.[9]

I wish to record that the first reactions of the American people to the collapse of the Soviet Russian empire were commendable. There was no popular jubilation, no wish to rub Russian noses in the dust, no public proclamations (except by some Republicans that their party had "won" the Cold War). But soon the temptation to extend American power into portions of the world emptied by another great power proved to be too alluring—in this case less because of popular nationalism than because of the officers of the American superstate.

In this there was not much difference between Republicans and Democrats. It was the government of Clinton (a man otherwise not much interested in foreign policy) that chose to extend the American military presence into Somalia, into the Caucasus, into the Balkans, etc. At the beginning of the twenty-first century, as America's third century began, there were perhaps more than eight hundred American "bases" all around the world. I doubt whether there was, or is, a single man or woman in the Pentagon or in the Department of State (or of course in the White House) who could list even half of them. Neither could the American people, ignorant of the extent of what this means. Most of them went on believing that they are a Chosen People, an exception not only to others but to history itself, that they were living in the greatest and freest and richest country in the world.

The decision of George W. Bush[10] and of his followers to go to war against Iraq was part and parcel of such beliefs—but with one ominous condition, perhaps without precedent. That decision was not the result of inadequate intelligence. (That the CIA tells presidents what they wish to hear was nothing new.) Nor was it the result of geopolitical calculation. The choice of that war was his and his advisers' belief that going into Iraq and crushing its miserable dictator in a quick war would be popular, resounding to a great and enduring advantage to his reputation and to the Republican Party's dominance in the foreseeable future.[11] There have been many American presidents who have chosen to go to war, for different reasons: but I know of no one who chose to go to war to enhance his popularity.[12] Three years passed and the war in Iraq turned unpopular. Yet the Democratic senators and congressman and presidential aspirants have been afraid to seem insufficiently nationalist.[13] They proclaimed their concern with Our Troops there; they did not ask why those troops were there at all. They, and popular discontent with the war, argued against its enormous financial costs and against the much less than enormous amount of blood shed there by Our Troops. They blamed the Iraqi government while they said nothing about the perhaps one hundred thousand deaths of Iraqi people, their monstrous sufferings perhaps largely caused by the American invasion and presence in that unfortunate country—an absence of concern different from American generosity extended to other defeated peoples in the past.[14]

During the past quarter-century the persistence of American popular nationalism grew together with something more recent: with the militarization of popular imagination. That has been inseparable from the growth of the American imperial presidency. Republicans and "conservatives" proclaim their opposition to Big Government; but they are the most aggressive proponents of enormous military expenditures and institutions, as if "defense" were not part of the "government."[15] A president's journey now, especially abroad, includes more than one thousand agents, officers, servants, the retinue of a superimperial progress, dwarfing what we know of the retinue of a Genghis Khan or that of Louis XIV.

"The president"—says Section 2 of Article II of the Constitution—"shall be commander in Chief of the Army and Navy of the United States, and of the militia of the several states, when called into the actual service of the United States." Thereafter that short paragraph lists other presidential powers that have nothing to do with military matters. The brevity of the mention of a commander in chief—it is less than a full sentence—suggests that the Founders did not attach enormous importance to that role. Thereafter presidents, including former generals, chose not to emphasize their military function during their presidential tenure, in accord with the American tradition of the primacy of civilian over military rule. Of their constitutional prerogatives they were of course aware. Lincoln would dismiss and appoint generals; Truman knew that he had the right to fire MacArthur. But none of the presidents who governed this country during its great wars kept insisting that they were commanders in chief—not Washington, not Lincoln, not Wilson, not Roosevelt. Until now.[16]

Around 1980 the militarization of the image of the presidency began—with Reagan, who had no record of military service, having spent World War II in Hollywood. There were his fervent, sentimental, and sometimes tearful expressions when meeting or speaking to American soldiers, sailors, airmen. There was, too, his easy and self-satisfied willingness to employ the armed forces of the United States in rapid and spectacular military operations against minuscule targets of "evil," against "enemies" such as Grenada, Nicaragua, Libya. The younger Bush, too, enjoyed immersing himself in the warm bath of jubilant approbation at large gatherings of selected soldiery.

When Ronald Reagan was given a salute by military personnel, he would return it, shooting his right hand up to his bare head, his happy smile suggesting that this was something he liked to do. This unseemly and unnecessary habit was adopted by Reagan's successors, including Clinton and especially George W. Bush, who stepped off his plane and cocked a jaunty salute. This gesture is wrong. Such a salute has always required the wearing of a uniform. But there is more to this than a corruption of military manners. There is something puerile in the Reagan and Clinton and Bush salute. It is the gesture of someone who likes playing soldier. It also represents an undue exaggeration of a president's military function. War is a serious matter, but like the boy-soldier salute, a sentimentalization of military matters is puerile. Television depictions of modern technological warfare, too, make it seem as if a military campaign were but a superb game, an International Super Bowl that Americans are bound to win—and with few or no human losses. ("We'll keep our fighting men and women out of harm's way"—a senseless phrase uttered by members of Clinton's government.)

This is something new in American history. When the Roman Republic gave way to empire, the new supreme ruler, Octavian (Augustus), chose to name himself not "rex," king, but "imperator," from which our words *emperor* and *empire* derive, even though its original meaning was more like commander in chief. Thereafter Roman emperors came to depend more and more on their military. History does not repeat itself, but some of its conditions do. Is this the destiny of the United States?[17]

I do not know. What I know is that, beyond military gamesmanship, puerility is a dangerous thing. There are, alas, many institutions in this country now, ranging from education to entertainment, that contribute to it, and powerfully so. But the sustenance of puerility may be even worse than decadence.[18] (After all, decadence is chock-full of dissolving maggots of maturity, of remnant memories that puerility does not possess.) A puerile presidency may be but one symptom of the devolution of this republic into a military superstate. Consider but one, again entirely new, development: the American government's hiring and empowering tens of thousands of "private" mercenary fighters, "security" forces unknown and unaccounted for by Congress, freed of the governance and discipline of traditional military authority. Or consider the accumulated and secret powers of the Central Intelligence Agency.

It was founded in 1947–48 for the purpose of coordinating intelligence previously gathered by different departments of the American government. Soon it assumed the power to arrange, direct, and perform secret operations[19] throughout the entire world (and above its skies), superseding the authority and functions of the Department of State, establishing its own secret bases and prison camps and other lawless activities abroad, largely unknown and unsupervised by the elected representatives of the American people.

"The sudden change from democracy," wrote the great Jakob Burckhardt 150 years ago, "will no longer result in the rule of an individual, but in the rule of a military corporation. And by it, methods will perhaps be used for which even the most terrible despot would not have the heart."[20]

Nationalism and militarism are popular sentiments. That does not minimize, it maximizes their importance, since the most powerful element in the history of a democracy is the accumulation not of materials but of opinions and sentiments. But that condition, in America, is not simple. There is the split-mindedness of so many Americans. (Split-mindedness, not schizophrenia: not a vertical division between what is conscious and less conscious; rather, the tendency to profess contradictory values within the same mind.) Americans tend to believe not only that they are a Chosen People[21] but also that what is good for America is good for the world: Yet at the same time they are not much interested in the world outside the United States. Many Americans admire their military unreservedly, they are willing to pay taxes for it at any time; yet they are not eager to be drafted for military service. Something of a split-mindedness prevails about their—so-called—materialism, too. Americans think that matter and money are most important, and that money is what most people most want,[22] but there are many kinds of evidences suggesting that for many Americans what matters is less their possession of money than their ability to spend it. Americans may be the least materialistic people in the world: there is enough evidence to argue this. However—there is now a fairly new condition, which is the spiritualization of matter: the intrusion of mind into matter, into the very structure of it.[23] The great and profound danger in America is not materialism but a false spiritualism running rampant.[24]

A historian cannot and must not predict what will happen: but he may at least essay what will not happen. Liberalism will not recover.[25] But the Gadarene rush of former liberals to the "conservative"—or, more precisely, to the nationalist—side, their ephemeral overweight in the American commerce of intellectual and political ideas and preferences, will not last long either. There is one great and grave fault in the thinking of American conservatives as well as of American liberals. This is their belief in (linear) Progress. The liberals', ever more strained, propaganda for the extension of limitless human "freedoms," their clinging to the Darwinist categories of evolution and "progress," not only compromises but goes counter to their once noble protection and defense of human dignity. The conservatives' propagation of American power throughout the world and, above it, into space, their thoughtless belief in the endless benefits of technology, amounts to a denial of every conservative view of human nature and of its limits.

Liberals adulate Science; conservatives adulate Technology.[26] No great difference there. Consider but the favorite "conservative," and "Christian," idea of what *they* call "creationism," their propagation of the phrase of Intelligent Design, that is: God as an "intelligent designer," as if He were a rocket scientist or a computer wizard. That most of our self-proclaimed Conservatives ignore—worse, they dismiss with contempt—true conservatism is reason enough to deny their very designation of themselves as conservatives.[27]

And yet, for the first time more and more Americans, some of them perhaps not quite consciously but more and more so, have begun to question the myth of endless mechanical and beneficial "Progress." They are still not an organized or a political minority, but they are not insignificant. They are concerned—after all, it involves their very lives—with what happens to their country and with their government's management and material destruction of nature (for which *environment* is a weak and stuttering word). They are the true conservatives, because of their respect for traditions, because of their authentic sincerity, incarnating a deep and pure spiritualism. Men and women such as Dorothy Day. Wendell Berry. George Kennan. Two of them are dead now but their influence will live on. I know some such people. They enliven my more and more isolated existence with hope. Even in American academic life a scatteration of true conservative probity has been evident for some time now. Some of the best American historians, thinkers, teachers, researchers, writers may be found—yes, they *ought* to be found—in the oddest places of this vast country, in little-known places, small colleges and universities, rather than in the repositories of Harvard or Yale or Princeton.[28]

"Mine is an odd destiny," Alexander Hamilton wrote to Gouverneur Morris in 1803. "Every day proves to me more and more that this American world was not made for me." It was not made for me either. Hamilton and I: we were not born here. I also know something that he did not know: the American handicap of a state and its doctrine born in the middle of the so-called Enlightenment, in the middle of the five hundred years of the so-called Modern Age that is now largely gone.

Still, there are moments, minutes, hours, when I can be happy. Here, even now. It could be worse.

It could be worse: but very good it is not.

There are dualities in every human being. One duality: my Hungarian-European and my Anglo-American selves. Readers, believe me: the first of these pairs may be *deeper* than the second, but it does not *dominate* the second. The American, Benjamin Franklin trumpeted, is a self-made man. Not more than a half-truth (and so many half-truths are worse than are lies). I am not a self-made American. I have not dismissed my ancestry. But I am not a Hungarian writer, though I still can and could be that. This is not a result of choosing a language for writing. It is a consequence of thinking. Writing is one result of thinking. Is thinking the result of feeling? Yes and no. Thinking involves a choice. Feeling may be the source of a choice but not its result. Ignore feeling. My mind is concerned with this, my adopted country, and with its history. It is, too, with my native country and with its history. Sometimes less. Seldom more.

When, on rare and memorable occasions, I was called a master of my native language, my mind was a tremble with sentiments of gratitude. When, on other rare and memorable occasions, I was called a master of English prose, I was proud beyond reason. In the introduction of my perhaps most extraordinary book, *A Thread of Years*, I wrote: "In the second part of each annualized chapterette, I challenge myself. *Myself*: because my interlocutor is my alter ego. He is not an imaginary person; he is not a composite or a confection of someone else. He is more commonsensical, more pragmatic, more direct, more down-to-earth than is the narrator of the vignette, and we argue, add, subtract, agree, disagree. . . . When the idea (or, rather, the plan) of such a construction first occurred to me I cannot tell. It may be that while the author of my vignettes and their occasional defendant is my European self, my challenger and debater is my American one. It may be: perhaps not. But it is no use to discuss this further."

I wrote half of my more than two dozen books during the past twenty years of my life. Their writing took me (and still takes me) about two years on the average. A "prolific" writer, people on occasion write or say.[29] I dislike that adjective. It is not a pretty one. In the *Oxford English Dictionary* it has not one pejorative meaning: still, I dislike it. That does not matter. What does matter is my alienation from my profession. Fourteen years ago, when I was made to resign (because of age) from teaching at my college, the then chairman of the history department of the University of Pennsylvania asked me to teach a single course in a single semester. I took up the assignment with pleasure, continuing it for three years. That history department consisted of forty-five professors, of whom I knew two. Soon it was obvious that none of the others desired to meet me. In my third and last semester I had memorable students, six of them, the seventh a faker. They surprised me with a gift of a bottle of fine French champagne on the last day of class. A few days later my wife brought me the telephone. I was in the garden, mowing. The new chairman of the department spoke haltingly, in an unsteady voice: she said that they had no place for me any longer. Of course I was disappointed: but disappointments so often turn out to be blessings. Now I had even more time and air and space for writing. A year or two later, a friend, a historian far away, rang me up to chat. He asked me how I was doing. A sudden thought, or a turn of phrase, sprang in my mind. "I have many things to complain about," I said, "but I have no reason to complain."[30]

Through fifty years of college teaching and writing, often I have run into ignorance, disdain, exclusion, professional snobbery, gray ice on other professors' faces! Professional academics are a kind of guild. Why should they not be uneasy with this strange presence in their guild? I have come from the outside as a very young man from a distant, small country in Europe, with academic credentials not entirely identical or even similar to the American PhD; I got a job and stayed on teaching in a small Catholic college of no unusual distinction. I thought that I would try to make my name known not dependent on the customary academic stepladder, that slippery and wooden *gradus ad Parnassum*, but by writing remarkable books. What books? Books on various subjects interesting for me, at times against the accepted ideas and categories of their current specialists.[32] Worse: as time went on, I attacked some of them; indeed, I attacked my very profession. I argued and wrote that history was, and is, not a Science: that often the "professional" category applied to historianship was imprecise; that so many academic historians were not even interested in history very much; what they were interested in was their historianship, their status within "the profession"—and not that "history" consists of and depends on words, without which "facts" have no meaning. Why, then, should I have expected the sympathy, let alone the embrace, of the guild?[33] Was I entitled to have my cake and eat it too? No. I remain aware of the pettiness, of the shortsightedness of professional academics. But *comprendre, c'est pardonner*: I respect and appreciate and, whenever I can, support those younger men and women struggling to enter the guild—if *guild* remains a proper word at all.

Once, about fifteen or so years ago, I overheard another professor talking about me: "He is a historian; but he is really a writer." (He said this with a slightly deprecatory tone; he did not know that I was standing within hearing distance of him.) I think I was—and I still am—amused, not wounded. Yes, I am a writer; and a historian who cannot write well enough cannot be a good historian. We have, and should have, no jargon. Our instrument is the common language. We write and teach and speak and think with words.

Around me, within thirty or forty miles, are at least five universities and dozens of colleges, staffed by tens of thousands of academic intellectuals. I know few of them. I have lived around here for more than sixty years; in this very place for fifty-four. There is one difference from what still existed, say, one generation ago. Then there were in my neighborhood some men and women who were not academics but were then called "intellectuals": people who bought and read books and periodicals, who had interests in art, who took some comfort or pride in their broad-mindedness. A class of opinion, rather than of society, they were. *Intellectual*, as a noun, appeared in the English language, in Britain and then in the United States, in the 1880s and 1890s. It was, oddly, an immigrant noun, a word and usage from Tsarist Russia, where intellectuals, no matter how few, were more or less recognizable men and women. I had not come from such a world: for a long time, through many decades, I bridled against being called An Intellectual: I found that many of the minds of such people were more narrow than they had thought themselves, or so broad as to be flat; I declared that I was a teacher and a writer and that was that. But during the past twenty or thirty years there came a change. Intellectuals in America, as a social class of opinion, have just about ceased to exist. There are a few intellectuals among academics, but of course there are many more academics who are not intellectual at all. I would have never thought that one day I should miss the presence of intellectuals around me; I do—a little—now.

The world of universities and of intellectual commerce at large is now more remote from me than it was before. But the subject of this book, and perhaps especially of this chapter, is not I but the world around me. And there great changes, transformations, have occurred. One of them is not wholly new. It began at least one hundred years ago. It is the decline of the written and of the printed word: the change from a verbal to a pictorial "culture": indeed, to the ways of thinking and seeing: the rising appearance of a new Middle or, rather, Dark Ages of symbols, pictures, images, abstractions. This has happened together with a breakdown of normal communications—in spite, or rather, because of the propaganda of an Information Age.[33]

And beneath and beyond these phenomena runs the tide of cynicism. For a long time many Americans, idealists as well as pragmatists, were optimistic about democracy, overestimating the potential intelligence of their people. But even an illusory idealism is preferable to a calculating cynicism. During the twentieth century the purveyors of education and of information and of entertainment, the managers of intellectual and artistic commerce, the publishers of printed matter, the manipulators of visual matter, and, worst of all, the administrators of American education, have established and solidified their careers and fortunes through a, to them "practical" but in reality cynical, underestimation of the potential intelligence of the American people, very much including their youth. There are myriad examples of this.

Readers of books: they still exist, scattered in some of the oddest nooks and crannies of this large country. But the breakdown of communications has affected them too. One of the outcomes of that is the rapid deterioration of attention, the nervous constriction of its span.[34] This includes academics and scholars. So many of them no longer buy books. Or even read them: they prefer to read, instead, reviews. Those too, they read fast, since their interest is seldom in the matter discussed: it is what "A" ventures, or dares, to say about "B."

It could be worse. This is a very big country. Not everywhere, and not always, does its cult of equality—constraining as it often is—imprison us into uniformity. Solitude and inattention are not everywhere, and not always destructive. By and large they have allowed (rather than permitted) me to invent my own occupation, my maverick profession and career, writing different books, each of them published by reputable firms, some of them reviewed here and there with some respect. What is much more important: they are noted by a scattering of readers, many of them young, some of them true "conservatives." My occasional encounters with them give me much pleasure. So, constrained but not entirely disallowed I am, by what has been "developing" around me.

In the same place, on the same piece of land, I have been living for fifty-four years now. This alone makes me different from my neighbors. I hardly know my closest neighbors now, nothing of their lives, of their characters, of their minds. We are parcels of different, increasingly different, worlds. The civilization to which I belonged, whose child I was, which I tried to prize and protect and reconstruct within this house, on these few acres, in this countryside, in this Pennsylvania, in these United States, in this world, has largely vanished. The last people who belonged to it, whom I knew, who were dear to me, have vanished too. I am a remnant, with less pride and more misery in my heart, by much what I hear and see. People with whom one would talk about some things, in a certain language, exist no more. It is not like those French aristocrats who fled after 1790 and then talked about life before 1789, the ancien régime: a few years later most of those men and women returned to their ancestral places. Now I think that I am the only one around me who has lived in the same place for almost sixty years. That circumstance may have earned me some respect, from some. But, by and large, it contributes to most of my new neighbors' sense of my un-Americanness. Pennsylvania is among the more sedate states of the Union. Its population has hardly increased and the average age is older than elsewhere. Yet the average Pennsylvanian now moves every four or five years. His mind depends on an abstract outside world. With his television and computer and Internet and two automobiles and at least two mobile telephones, he is connected to a world, to his American world, more than ever before. These things render him different from his restless ancestors. Americans have always been restless. But not like they are now, moving from suburb to suburb.

Human nature does not change. Human character does not much change either. But it is malleable. What changes is human behavior, because of thinking: or, rather, because of acquired habits of thinking. I wrote umpteen times that people do not *have* ideas, they *choose* them. To this let me add that, almost always, people will adjust their ideas to circumstances, rather than adjust circumstances to their ideas. Circumstances are what I am thinking and writing about. Some of these circumstances being that I know little or nothing about my close neighbors now, and they know little or nothing about me. I would not mind knowing a little more about them, but this is not reciprocal. I do not know what goes on and very little of what exists inside their houses. They do not know, or wish to know, what goes on in mine. My interest in them may be larger than theirs in me, but that is not the point. They know very little about their other neighbors too. This is the world that now exists around me.

Thirty years ago about six thousand people lived in my township. I knew the names of perhaps half of them. Not now.

I know that I can depend on one, perhaps two, of my close neighbors in an emergency, in the good old American way, for help. That, too, could be worse. Still, most of them, married couples, are away for most of the day, even on weekends. That circumstance—or call it a condition—knocks away the foundation of the American suburban aspirations of forty or fifty years ago. Those had a sentimental foundation, but then that is so with all that seem (but only seem) to be materialist aspirations in America. It was the ideal of a house, one's own, on a small grassy plot, away from a packed city and its crowded traffic, a sunny life, with new neighbors and friends, close but not separated from each other by high fences and walls: an ideal for a woman even more than for a man (the latter having to learn some lawn work and carpentry). Very soon it did not turn out that way. American womanhood in the suburbs turned out to be lonely, in many ways lonelier than the lives of pioneer wives in the middle of empty prairies in a sod house. Sooner or later, every young wife in the suburbs decided to go out somewhere, to be "employed," to "work" (as if keeping a house, feeding and caring for a family, were not work).[35] More than two hundred years ago Samuel Johnson was—and now remains, as almost always—right. "To be happy at home is the end of all human endeavor." To be happy outside the home is now the aim of much American endeavor—certainly for the young, and for not so young "adults" too.

Sweeping generalizations these are: but then generalizations, like brooms, ought to sweep . . . We had friends, most of them old Americans, not academics, not intellectuals, but men and women who read a little, traveled a little, cultivated their gardens (not a little), with whom I and my wife could talk about houses and gardens and places and people and things, with our common—not identical, but common—sensibilities. Many of them had what Goethe once called "die Höflichkeit des Herzens," the courtesies of the heart. Then they began to die, they went away and died. Thirty years ago we had dinner parties in their houses or in ours. Now we have friends for dinner once or twice a year. Family dinners of course more often. This, too, could be worse.

One more example of the breakdown of communications: my—our—everyone's—divorce, distance, separation from Philadelphia. More than a half-century ago I and my wife chose to live in Chester County: still, we were Philadelphians.

The movement of the middle classes to the suburbs had begun, but a sense of Philadelphianness prevailed. Those who lived beyond the city traveled there each weekday to work, as did my first wife then. We, and many others, were drawn to the city because of its stores, shops, institutions, theaters, the orchestra. Much of Philadelphia I loved. A quarter of a century later I wrote a book about Philadelphia, *Philadelphia: Patricians and Philistines, 1900–1950* (1981). But Philadelphia is a faraway, a foreign city now. Faraway: because of the very "progress"—that is: the partial collapse of communications, and of physical transportation. The godawful Schuylkill Expressway, built in the 1950s, was constructed to bring suburbs and city closer and closer together. The very opposite happened. Soon it made normal driving into the city difficult; and thereafter nearly impossible, impacted as it is almost every hour of the day and night. Foreign too: no one I know works in the city any longer. No one I know does Christmas shopping in Philadelphia. No one I know subscribes to the Orchestra.[36] I know but one friend who lives in the city. I no longer rate a Philadelphia telephone directory: if I need a number there, I have to call Information. There is a monthly magazine, *Philadelphia*, of thirty years' standing now. "Standing"—or rather, lying in dentists' offices. When I pick it up I recognize not one person and not one place in it. It might as well be a magazine of Atlanta or Seattle or Dallas. The city of Philadelphia has become alien.[37]

True nostalgia is a desire less for a time than for a place. True patriotism is a love for one's country and for its traditions. Philadelphia did not have much of a literary tradition, but it had considerable and even great painters, from Peale to Eakins. But there was a group of eastern Pennsylvania, not Philadelphia, painters and paintings—what and how they painted, the small world that they reflected and represented widens my tired old eyes and clutches my heart. They are, loosely called, the Pennsylvania Impressionists. Around 1900–1910 they began to gather, they chose to settle, live, and work, in what was then still an entirely rural landscape on the shore and in the mild valleys of the Delaware, in eastern Bucks County, Pennsylvania. Among them were Redfield, Garber, Lothrop, Folinsbee, Baum, Leith-Ross, Coppedge, Meltzer, Schofield, Rosen, Spencer, Taylor, Van Roekens, Witherspoon. Two were women; two of them Englishmen: for whatever reason, they chose to live here. Others had come here from the flat American Midwest. Was theirs an "Artists' Colony"? Yes and no. They had nothing in common with the intellectual self-consciousness, with the self-proclaimed radicalism of the Provincetown Cape Cod people circa 1913 (often referred in American intellectual or art history as "the Little Renaissance"—well, it was very little indeed). Most of them, with their gnarled hands, were master woodworkers and carpenters too, craftsmen able to build houses and barns. After they lifted their nimble fingers from their brushes, their eyes moved from the exquisite nuances of their palettes and colors to the straight, hard, precise fitting of grooves and planks and boards. Around 1910 Edward Redfield wrote that "Bucks County was a place where an independent, self-sufficient man could make a living from the land, bring up a family and still have the freedom to paint as he saw fit." How admirable! How American! In a once country. At a once time.

Yes, they were Impressionists, but not simply American imitators or successors of the famous great French painters before them. They had one thing in common with these French masters, or with other Impressionists all over the world. It was a new way of painting because of a new comprehension of seeing (a comprehension rather than a conscious knowledge; Pascal: "We understand more than we know"), an understanding of the limitations of the human mind and eye that might actually enrich the capacity, the depth, and the beauty of human vision. Or, in other words: a participation[38] in the world one sees. Whence their suggestive rendering of the colors and waters and seasons and air, of the farmhouses and barns and trees and paths and hillsides around Cuttaloosa or New Hope or Lumberville. Some of their paintings are ineffably beautiful. I am not a critic of art, not even of their art. My subject is not their method or even their accomplishment. It is their superb and modest present of a world, of an American world that is now gone, a portion of a world with its provincialness and plenitude, including plenty of decency and goodness,[39] of landscapes, God- *and* man-made. A landscape is not wholly "nature," it is God-made but with signs of a human presence. There were no paintings of landscapes in the Middle Ages. We have come to see the beauty of our world differently now.

They lived in the country, in a small portion of the Pennsylvania American country. They were among the last incarnations of a civilization that had begun to sink in their lifetime, at the end of the Bourgeois Age, and of the American bourgeois interlude. They would be surprised to be called "bourgeois," which was a curse word employed not only by revolutionaries but by intellectuals and artists during more than one hundred years; but they were bohemians not at all. Well, their beautiful small world was going, too, together with them. Around 1935 Bucks County and New Hope were discovered by the New York theatrical and intellectual aggregation. Soon afterward most of the painters were dead and gone. And yet—about sixty years later their heritage survived the noisy, fretful, self-consciously cynical world of theater directors and their writers. The bucket of art criticism may be a pit of snakes; and yet the Pennsylvania Impressionists are beginning to be rediscovered. So it could be, it could have been worse. As for me, it is to the provincial world they reflected and represented to which my heart belongs.

More than two hundred years ago, Edmund Burke wrote in his *Reflections on the Revolution in France*:

> To be attached to the subdivision, to love the little platoon we belong to in society, is the first principle (the germ as it were) of public affections. It is the first link in the series by which we proceed towards a love to our country and to mankind.

A few years ago Wendell Berry wrote:

> My devotion thins as it widens. I care more for my household than for the town of Port Royal, more for the town of Port Royal than for the County of Henry, more for the County of Henry than for the State of Kentucky, more for the State of Kentucky than for the United States of America. But I do not care more for the United States of America than for the world.

I care more for my household than for Schuylkill Township, more for Schuylkill Township than for Chester County, more for Chester County than for the State of Pennsylvania, more for the State of Pennsylvania than for the United States of America, and I do not care more for the United States of

America than for the world: at least for the world of what remains of Western civilization.

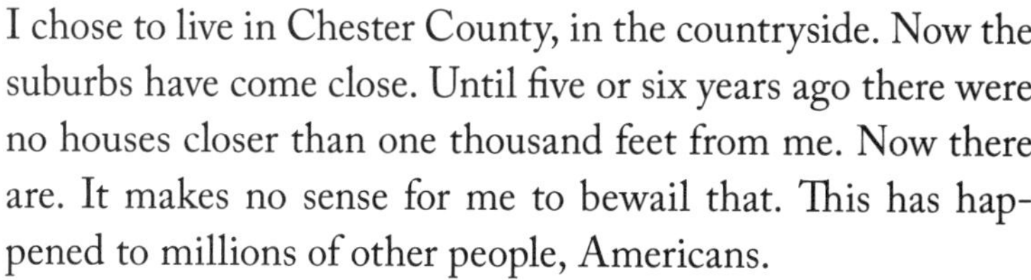

I chose to live in Chester County, in the countryside. Now the suburbs have come close. Until five or six years ago there were no houses closer than one thousand feet from me. Now there are. It makes no sense for me to bewail that. This has happened to millions of other people, Americans.

I still live on three acres that belonged to my first wife's ancestors for almost two hundred and fifty years. After 1955 those other 136 acres to my east, with some old buildings, were no longer of her family. They were largely unchanged by a new owner and his second wife and their children who inherited it but did not live there. Ten years ago they sold it to large developers. Now there are new more-than-one- or two-million-dollar houses, three of them now less than a thousand feet from us, visible in the winter. But it could have been worse. I was able, as an official of the township,[40] to advise and convince the owners not to challenge the township zoning ordinance: I told them that that would cost them many years and much money. Whence I have now three new neighbors, not thirty.

A few years after 1955, on winter evenings, I read through, arranged, preserved, some of my wife's ancestors' papers. I also cared for the family cemetery. One of my wife's few prominent ancestors had established a family cemetery a mile to the east from here. The first family graves there go back to the eighteenth century. The last family member buried there was my father-in-law in 1955; I drew his gravestone to resemble some of the other old ones. Later I became one of the trustees of the

Anderson Burial Ground. There were no wreaths, no visitors. The gate was broken and the stone wall cracked. The upkeep cost some work and money. One of the trustees died. Eventually I remained the one in charge. I did not do much.

It could have been worse. About eight years ago I convinced the Supervisors of the Township to take over the cemetery, assuring its perpetual upkeep.[41] Repairs were made, a historical plaque was installed, on which are embossed the names and dates (I had been able to reconstruct them) of twenty-one of the twenty-two men and women and children buried there through two hundred years. On November 4, 2006, there was a ceremony. The plaque, handsomely made, was dedicated. The day commemorated, too, the founding of Schuylkill Township 180 years before, its separation from Charlestown Township promoted by Isaac Anderson then. I was named the first Distinguished Citizen of Schuylkill Township. A resolution honoring me by the Pennsylvania House of Representatives was handed to me. It was a very American ceremony, with an American willingness of the heart. I embraced Norman and Ted, two of the township supervisors, my old friends.

About ten years ago, at the very end of *A Thread of Years*, I wrote: "It's all over for this work, for this book" (which ended with the year 1969, which I saw as a milestone marking the end of Anglo-American civilization), and probably for most of the world that I (and you, my alter ego) cherish and stick to, but God is infinitely good, since it is He and not Voltaire who allows and even prods us to cultivate our garden. And what a beautiful afternoon it is! Look at the color of the water. And at Stephanie's yellow and blue flowers. That heap of pots there is her job, but there are the heads of my asparagus appearing and the raspberries are coming out. Let's try to coax her out of the kitchen and busy ourselves there. What a beautiful afternoon this is!

Ten years later Stephanie is dead and the asparagus and the raspberries do poorly, if at all. But there is Pamela's beauteous mass of yellow and red flowers. Our terrace, our garden, our house is an island in the midst of an encroaching tide of suburbs and cement.[42] But there is another island, too: a real one, out in the stream, ever more in our sight, growing month by month. What was only a few years ago a large placid shallow lake is filling up, with silt, from "developments," more and more of them, upstream. Man-made, irremovable, incorrigible. In a few years our once lake will become a stream narrowing each winter, each year.

Still there is that forest of greenery on the other side of the water; and on this side, our grass descends to it, emerald and gilt under the sun, spinach-green after the shadows advance across it. One now unforgettable evening, about a dozen years ago, I suddenly decided to row down to my friends, the Reeves, two miles away. So I went, with the plashing of my oars the only sound, except for one far cry of a loon. I rowed into their inlet and clambered up on their steep overgrown slope. We had a drink. I started to row homeward. I was alone, in the middle of the reservoir. Soon I saw not a single light. Alone, on that dark indigo water, as if one hundred miles away from any town, out in some wilderness, under a sickle moon. I was full of gratitude for what God and this country had allowed me, for this silent world where I belonged, where I had chosen to live. A mile ahead, after the bend, I saw the lights of our house. In twenty minutes I was home.

Another night, eight years into the twenty-first century, another night falls now, after another day. The twilight of senility falls on my mind. Ahead of me, attracting me to the blissful solitude of sleep, that island within islands. Strange islands my dreams are![43] I sleep eight, nine hours every night. When I wake up my dreams surround me, like clouds weighing down. They have to disperse before I face the new day—which, at my age, is no longer "le vierge, le vivace, et le bel aujourd'hui." There are no dreams without thinking. There is no thinking without memories. We can have no memories, no dreams of the future, of any future.

Old age is a shipwreck.[44] It could be worse. I am alone; but not alone. One day or one night I will die. But remembered I shall be, by my wife, by my children, by my grandchild, by my stepchildren, by my remaining friends, by my platoon.[45]

One last summary chart of my itinerary. What a strange life I have had, what a strange solitary ship, what a strange ship, what strange seas! When I was young, did I, could I imagine that I'd live this long? Well, whatever my genes, my life in America made this possible for me. Had I remained in Hungary I would not now be alive. I left my country when I was young, at the age of twenty-two,[46] because I set my sight to the west, The West. I thought that the victory of America, of Britain, of the "West," meant restoration as much as progress: a restoration of the conservative and liberal freedoms and institutions that Hitler and the Germans and others had been ready to raze. Decline of The West, some day: but still a long sunny afternoon of human freedom and human dignity, perhaps even for many decades, during which because of their barbaric stupidities Russia's empire and Communism will not last. I was right about the latter but that was about all. Soon I recognized—more, I became ever more deeply, ever more painfully aware of—what separated and still separates me from almost all Americans I know. This is my awareness that I—we—have now lived not only in the twilight but beyond the end of an entire great historical epoch, of the great European and bourgeois age of about five hundred years, of which the establishing of the United States of America was an inexorable part.[47] That kind of knowledge behooves me, a historian. But it is also engraved in my heart.

There is no eternal return in history. It is not like a pendulum that swings back. There are not even ephemeral returns. Some inclinations do reappear, in circumstances that are new. There always has been a strain in the American mind that is older than the Enlightenment, that was (and is) contrary to the Enlightenment. I have called it the medieval strain in America: the particularly American split-minded coexistence of medieval with super-modern habits of mind.[48] Seven or eight hundred years ago the medieval world was incapable of facing the condition that contradictory matters could coexist within the same accepted doctrines or dogmas. Johan Huizinga, great historian, wrote in *The Passing of the Middle Ages*: "A too systematic idealism gives a certain rigidity of the conception of the world. . . . Men disregarded the individual qualities and the fine distinctions of things, deliberately and of set purpose, in order always to bring them under some general principle. . . . What is important is the impersonal. The mind is not in search of individual realities, but of models, examples, norms. . . . There is in the Middle Ages a tendency to ascribe a sort of substantiality to abstract concepts." All of this was and is as true of Puritans as it is of Disneyland, of Superman as of the public relations man, of most American Fundamentalists and Evangelicals as of many American Catholics,[49] of television as of the American War against Evil. Around us are now symptoms, signs of a new Dark Ages—except that history does not repeat itself.

That is, too—and this goes beyond America—why the deep crisis of Christianity and perhaps especially of the Roman Catholic Church[50] is not soluble through a return to medievalism, or to the Old Mass, or to new catechisms—no matter how the new medieval habits of mind, with their powerful but superficial sureties, may again attract masses of the faithful. The Church, my church, must now reconcile itself to be a church of a minority of the truly believing[52]—as it was, of course, in entirely different circumstances and with entirely different prospects after the age of the catacombs eighteen hundred or so years ago. The Church must remain a single, lonely lighthouse of human comprehension, of wisdom, a proponent of love. For God's (and the own) sake, Christians must steel themselves against temptations of popularity and success, against actors who may become Anti-Christs, kissing babies, blessing believers, announcing that they are great champions of prosperity and heroic warriors again evil. Such thoughts have often led me to think about the great division at the second coming of Christ, at the end of the world when Christians will be divided into a large conformist majority and a pitiful, suffering, and believing minority, just as were Jews so divided two thousand years ago, at the first coming of Christ.[53] That does not belong here. What may belong here is the despondent cry of a deep-thinking contemporary of ours, the Russian Tatyana Tolstoya, perhaps particularly relevant to the recovering Russian Orthodox now, but alas, too, of so many in the West: "We have no faith: we're afraid to believe, because we're afraid that we'll be deceived." I think that I am not afraid to believe—perhaps because I am a gambler.

Notes

Chapter I: History as Literature

1 Blake: "A Truth that's told with bad intent / Beats all the Lies you can invent."

2 Peter Burke, ed., *A New Kind of History: From the Writings of Febvre*, trans. K. Folca (New York: Harper & Row, 1973), 32–33.

3 One example: Churchill—not a modest writer—in the preface of his *The Second World War*: "I do not describe [my record] as history, for that belongs to another generation. But I claim with confidence that it is a contribution to history which will be of service for the future." Well, Churchill (as in some of his other books) was something more than a categorizable "amateur." (At the very time I am writing this, I am reading *Winston's War, 1940–1945* by Max Hastings, on the same tremendous subject: it is first-class, a worthy companion to Churchill's own six volumes—and, again, not written by an academic.)

4 About this, see my *The Hitler of History*, 1997.

5 "How many professional historians are there who would so modestly, so elegantly, and so knowledgably include a portrait by a novelist at the outset of your book? Hardly any." (My letter to Kennan, February 18, 1990.) "My own efforts to write diplomatic history taught me that there is no such thing as an objective historical reality outside 'the eye of the

beholder'—none, at least, that would be accessible to the human understanding—there is only the view taken of it by the individual historian, the value of which varies with the qualities—the honesty, the scrupulousness, the imagination, and the capacity for empathy—of the historian himself. This is why I view every work of narrative history as a work of the creative imagination, like the novel, but serving a somewhat different purpose and responsive to different, more confining rules" (Letter to Kennan to me, July 27, 1984).

6 One hundred fifty years ago, Trollope (in *The Claverings*): "As for reading . . . men and women believe the work is, to be, of all works, the easiest. . . . Alas, if the habit be not there, of all tasks it is the most difficult. If a man has not acquired the habit of reading till he be old, he shall sooner in his old age learn to make shoes than learn the adequate use of a book."

7 Max Beerbohm wrote this epigrammatic witticism about the 1880s: "To give an accurate and exhaustive account of that period would need a far less brilliant pen than mine." (A rare example of a good half-truth.) About the 1890s the American essayist and amateur historian Thomas Beer is his *The Mauve Decade*, incarnating an insatiable and intelligent curiosity, knew not only how but what to read, whence the unusual quality of his book.

8 Dabblers in the history of ideas should note that Carr's book of 1961 nearly coincided with Thomas Kuhn's *The Structure of Scientific Revolutions*, 1962, a worthless book in which the vocabulary substitutes for thought and which slides into Subjectivism, though it does not quite dare to espouse it while suggesting that science is but the result of scientists, the result "of a consensus of the scientific community."

9 Participation involves memory, and also inspiration. Huizinga: "There is in our historical consciousness an element of great importance that is best defined by the term historical sensation. One might also call it historical contact. . . . This contact with the past, a contact which it is impossible to determine or analyse completely . . . is one of the many ways given to man to reach beyond himself, to experience truth. The object of this feeling is not people as individuals. . . . It is hardly an image which our mind forms. . . . If it takes on a form at all this remains composite and vague: an *Ahnung* [sense] of streets, houses, as sounds and colours or people moving or being moved. There is in this manner of contact with the past the absolute conviction of reality. . . . The historical sensation is not the sensation of living the past again but of understanding the world as one does when listening to music." (*The Task of Cultural History*, VII, 71). Professor Kossmann at the Huizinga centennial conference, 1972: "I find it difficult to understand what exactly Huizinga was trying to describe in these passages." I don't.

10 "It is not only that Hitler had considerable intellectual talents. He was also courageous, self-assured, on many occasions steadfast, loyal to his friends and to those working for him, self-disciplined and modest in his physical wants. What this suggests ought not be misconstrued, mistaken,

or misread. It does not mean: lo and behold! Hitler was only 50 percent bad. Human nature is not like that. A half-truth is worse than a lie, because a half-truth is not a 50 percent truth: it is a 100 percent truth and a 100 percent untruth mixed together. In mathematics, with its rigidly fixed and immobile numbers, 100 plus 100 makes 200; in human life 100 plus 100 makes *another* kind of 100. Life is not constant: it is full of black 100s and white 100s, warm 100s and cold 100s, 100s that are growing and 100s that are shrinking" (43–44).

Chapter 2: American "Exceptionalism"

1 One example: the Republican Party (as well as most American conservatives) having become increasingly populist during the second half of the twentieth century.

2 As late as 1950 there was not one American political figure who would declare himself as a "conservative." (Senator Robert A. Taft in 1950: "I am not a conservative but an old fashioned liberal." As late as 1951 Senator Joseph McCarthy on one occasion called himself a "liberal." But in 1960 Eisenhower, on occasion, called himself "conservative." 1964: Goldwater, the presidential nominee of the Republican Party, declares that he is a conservative. 1980: Ronald Reagan, a divorced movie actor, elected by a huge majority, a proclaimed conservative. In 1955 William F. Buckley began his *National Review* on a shoestring. Twenty-five years later *National Review* had more subscribers than *The Nation* and the *New Republic* combined etc.

3 In 1949 the only opponents of NATO and of American commitments in Western Europe were the few remnant American communists and their fellow travelers on one end, and the remnant isolationist Republicans on the other end of the American political spectrum.

4 When I arrived in the United States in 1946, I was amazed and impressed by the coverage of Europe I could read every morning in the *New York Times*. Now I open the newspaper and the first half dozen pages of its International News section are always about places in Asia and Africa.

Chapter 3: The Germans' Two Wars: Heisenberg and Bohr

1 This young man with great powers of imagination and talent whom I, for one, have come to dislike because of his often arrogant and sinuous cleverness.

2 Winston Churchill, not yet in the British government, was told of the importance of the Berlin discovery in the summer of 1939; but his advisers (especially Professor F. A. Lindemann, later to become Lord Cherwell)

concluded, like Bohr, that the making of a bomb would be excessively costly and impractical. In retrospect, Churchill found this August 1939 memorandum important enough to include in the first volume of his Second World War history, *The Gathering Storm*, 1949, 386–87.

3 The letter did not reach Roosevelt until October; it was a second letter given to Alexander Sachs, the abovementioned financier, signed by Einstein (again drafted by Szilard and Wigner) on March 7, 1940, that brought about the secret support by the American government, culminating in its results five years later.

4 *At the End of an Age*, 88.

5 Helmut Rechenberg, "Kopenhagen 1941 und die Natur des deutschen Uranporkjektes," manuscript, p. 7 (my translation). Rechenberg is the director of the Heisenberg-Institut (and Archive) in Munich.

6 With one possible exception: see Weizsaecker's visit to Copenhagen in March 1941, page 120.

7 He was tried in Nuremberg in 1948 and was thereafter acquitted. One of his sons, Richard von Weizsaecker, an honorable and intelligent man, was elected president of (West) Germany in 1984.

8 The dates of the conference (September 18–23) did not exactly coincide with Heisenberg's stay (September 16–21) in Copenhagen.

9 Did Weizsaecker in March bring some kind of greeting or message from Heisenberg to Bohr in Copenhagen? Probably, but I have seen no evidence of that.

10 In Helmut Rechenberg, "Documentation and Reminiscences of the Bohr/Heisenberg Meeting in 1941," typescript; also in http://werner-heisenberg.unh.edu/copenhagen.htm.

11 I think this was Miss Ray, the Bohr children's nanny.

12 That noon at a reception and lunch at the German legation, Heisenberg was pleased that the American minister, a lady, was there and talked animatedly with her German host. The letter continues on Saturday night.

13 She was already a refugee in Stockholm when Heisenberg wrote her on the occasion of her sixtieth birthday, "[You have] enriched our science and thereby our entire lives," thanking her "for having this work in Germany, and for all you have done for German physics." This emphasis on Germany disappointed Meitner. Ruth Lewin Sime, *Lise Meitner: A Life in Physics* (Berkeley: University of California Press, 1996), 226–26.

14 She meant "unforgivable." Sime, *Lise Meitner,* 310.

15 Quoted in the *New York Times*, April 24, 2004.

16 Another duality: he did not wish Germany to lose; yet once or twice during the war he wrote or talked about an international (more precisely: supranational) community of scientists' moral concern about the applications of science for the sake of mankind.

17 Thomas Powers, *Heisenberg's War* (New York: Knopf, 1993), 106–7, recounting Reiche's recollections in 1961.

18 They include Bohr's visit from German-occupied Denmark to neutral Stockholm in the spring of 1941.

19 Letter of November 11, 1940, in *Liebe Eltern! Briefe aus kritischer Zeit 1918 bis 1945*, edited by his daughter Anna Maria Hirsch-Heisenberg (Munich: Langen/Müller, 2003), 313. "What do you think now that Chamberlain has died? I cannot but think with sympathy of a man who truly wanted peace but whose politics ended in a total shipwreck. . . . The English have it very tough now, but the death of one man means little in politics."

20 Alas, this went together with Heisenberg's dismissal of other Eastern European nations, as he said on one occasion, "who are not able to govern themselves."

21 Quoted in Sime, *Lise Meitner*, 303. See also the last paragraph of this chapter.

Chapter 5: The Origins of the Cold War

1 This accorded with the view of his wife, whose character and personality were very different from his, affecting their marital relations. Yet that was one of the instances when Eleanor's and Franklin's views of the world were more in accord than were their personalities.

2 I attempted to describe and emphasize this (including his fatal errors) in my June 1941: Hitler and Stalin. On one occasion, in August 1944, Molotov said to Stalin: Germany will try to make peace with Churchill and Roosevelt. Stalin answered: "Right, but Roosevelt and Churchill won't agree."

3 Drew Pearson, *Diaries, 1939–1959*, ed. Tyler Abell (New York: Holt, Rinehart, Winston, 1974), 134.

4 *My Dear Mr. Stalin: The Complete Correspondence of Franklin D. Roosevelt and Joseph V. Stalin*, ed. Susan Butler (New Haven: Yale University Press, 2005), 62.

5 The—temporary—American "deal" with Darlan dictated by necessity at that time, was violently criticized by liberals, leftists, and Communists throughout the world.

6 Butler, *My Dear Mr. Stalin*, 97. "Respectful": note Stalin's language to Roosevelt on another occasion (December 2, 1944) about Russian relations with France: "I ask your advice on this question as well," ibid, 270. In 1971 Harriman, angered by Dean Acheson's rather self-serving account of himself and Roosevelt and Truman (in an interview in the British journal *The Listener*), spoke to Arthur Schlesinger Jr., at length, which the latter found important enough to reproduce almost verbatim in his *Journals, 1952–2000* (New York: Penguin, 2007), 335–36. "FDR was basically right in thinking he could make progress in personal relations

with Stalin. My only difference with him was that he was more optimistic about how much progress he could make. Stalin was very much impressed with Roosevelt; you could almost say that he was in awe of Roosevelt. . . . I don't know what would have happened if FDR had lived. I only know that things would not have been the same. . . . Of course Roosevelt had his defects. . . . Sometimes he kept talking because he didn't want to give the other fellow a chance to talk. Sometimes he was overly naïve."

7 Butler, *My Dear Mr. Stalin*, 322–23.

8 The main printed sources of this episode are Max Waibel, *1945: Kapitulation in Norditalien* (Basel: Helbing & Lichtenhahn, 1981); Klaus-Dietmark Henke, *Die amerikanische Besetzung Deutschlands* (Munich: Oldenbourg, 1995); Bradley D. Smith and Elena Agarossi, *Operation Sunrise* (New York: Basic Books, 1979); and Allen Dulles, *The Secret Surrender* (New York: 1966), the last one considerably self-serving and insubstantial.

9 Henke, *Die amerikanische Besetzung Deutschlands*, 676; Waibel, 1945, 28, 31, 106, 107–8; see also Christopher Woods, "A Tale of Two Armistices," in K. G. Robertson, ed., *War, Resistance, and Intelligence: Essays in Honour of M. R. D. Foot* (London: Leo Cooper, 1999), 1–18, about C. R. D. Mallaby, a British SOE officer in Italy; also my *Hitler of History*, chap. 5.

10 Archbishop (soon to be Cardinal) von Galen in Münster, from whom the British had expected much because of his occasionally brave anti-Nazi sermons, on the first Sunday after Münster had fallen to the British referred in his sermon to these "foreign soldiers in our midst."

11 Morgenthau's and Dulles's subsequent careers are telling. In July 1945 President Truman got rid of Morgenthau, who presumed to be important enough to be one of Truman's advisers at the coming Potsdam summit conference. Dulles (whose brother John Foster was close to "America First" in 1940, and was a committed Republican, eventually becoming Eisenhower's secretary of state in 1952) became the head of the mighty Central Intelligence Agency, successor of the Office of Strategic Services. It may be said, without much exaggeration, that the Dulles brothers charted the course of the American ship of state during most of the 1950s.

12 For example, by the Polish ambassador to Washington, the excellent Jan Ciechanowski (see his *Defeat in Victory* [New York, 1947]).

13 Indeed, the Russian representative in the Allied Control Commission in Athens was instructed to refrain from meeting the Greek Communists. Meanwhile, as during the Darlan episode, American (and also British) liberals, Leftists, and Communists excoriated the British for their "imperialist interventions."

14 Seven years later, and one year before his death, in March 1952, Stalin suddenly offered something like a "neutral" and united Germany—

for the purpose of preventing what he feared: an American-German alliance.

15 In 1946 the Republican Party made large gains in the congressional elections. Its slogan in the campaign—"Had Enough?"—was more than clever. It suggested: enough of the New Deal, enough of Rooseveltism, enough of liberal illusions and of Communistic influences, enough of all of the propaganda during the Second World War. Etc.

16 "The Warsaw Uprising [in August 1944] was, I thought, the point at which, if we had never done so before, we should have insisted on a thoroughgoing exploration of Soviet intentions with regard to the future of the remainder of Europe." *George F. Kennan and the Origins of Containment, 1944–1946: The Kennan-Lukacs Correspondence* (Columbia: University of Missouri, 1997), 31.

17 As he allowed in one, only one, instance: that of Finland.

18 Church in 1950: the Soviets fear our friendship even more than they fear our enmity.

19 In 1944 to De Gaulle (see pages 169–170); on New Year's Eve in 1952 to his secretary John Colville: by the 1980s "Eastern Europe [would be] assuredly free of Communism."

Chapter 7: A Tocqueville Tide

1 "The nations of our time cannot escape equality of status; but it depends on themselves whether that equality will lead them to slavery or liberty, to enlightenment or barbarism, to prosperity or to wretchedness."

Chapter 8: The World Around Me: My Adopted Country

1 Diary (hereafter D.) January 19, 2001. "I never much liked the term Enlightenment, and now many of its illusions are gone. There is one exception where the word applies: the eventual opening of libraries, archives, records. Not fresh air and fresh light but more air and more light from those documents and papers. However: this too has been a passing phase. With the arrival of telecommunications of all kinds, and central intelligence agencies, etc., more and more things now remain and will remain unrecorded or unaccessible, unavailable, unreconstructable . . ."

2 D. August 17, 2004. "George Bush (the present President's father) told the American Olympic team in Athens to be sportsmanlike, to behave 'with class.' Class! that present, and stupid, usage of the word from the mouth of someone whom Americans describe—wrongly—as a 'patrician' or 'aristocrat.' This is the same man who speaks of his grandchildren as 'grandkids.' No gentleman would have ever used such a word."

3 D. June 6, 2004. "Result of civilizational degeneration: while a young fool would still not mind it if someone would call him a gentleman, no young woman now wants to be called a lady."

4 The real and only "modern" decade was the 1920s, not the 1960s. The latter was but the last, exaggerated, and often superficial application of the former.

5 As the 1960s proceeded, with many murders, there was an ocean of aroused concern with "violence": but the problem was not violence; it was savagery.

6 D. January 27, 2001. "Reading Englishmen and Englishwomen who were contemporaries of Spengler, say, about 1928. Yes, they were tired, and imperial Britain had begun to crumble. But, with all of his gigantic vision: was Spengler more intelligent than they were? Yes and no. Or: no rather than yes. Their way of speaking was better than Spengler's, which was not only a matter of language but of style too. Moreover, Spengler was no triumph of character. . . . He had a Cyclopean eye. But he was much less civilized than these tired Englishmen and Englishwomen, and I do not only mean his manners (though that is also telling). They may have been—they were—over-civilized. Spengler was over-cultured. And here my deep conviction: civilization is more important than culture, esp. than 'Kultur.'"

7 D. May 12, 2002. "Kierkegaard: 'People hardly ever make use of the freedom which they have, for example, freedom of thought; instead they demand freedom of speech as compensation.'"

8 D. August 19, 2004. "I know two rigid and near-extreme conservatives in this neighborhood. Their children are among the worst behaved. That too is telling."

D. February 16, 2002. "High-school students in a Kansas town stole their homework papers from the Internet and presented them entirely as their own. Their teacher, a young woman, 26, failed about twenty of them. The principal and the school board decided to restore the marks and to dismiss her. I am inclined to think that the school board people and the parents and the principal who insisted on her dismissal and on changing the students' grades are Republicans and Conservatives . . ."

9 D. April 14, 2003. "A Philadelphia radio personality, stupid, chauvinistic, fast-talking, calls me for a short telephone interview. He asks me: 'Come on! Hasn't Reagan single-handedly brought down the Soviet Union?' I: 'Yes, and Jefferson Davis won the Civil War.' He is furious and hangs up."

10 D. September 14, 2001. "Three days ago: the fanatics' planes smashing into the New York towers and the Pentagon. I am appalled by Bush. His first reaction: calling the perpetrators 'cowards.' Fanatics and murderers, yes. Cowards: not. Were Genghis Khan, Ivan, Hitler, etc., cowards? Alas, they were not. Bush likes the word: 'War.' Declare war, and against whom?"

11 D. October 11, 2001. "92% approval of Bush. . . . Walpole about the Tories 260 years ago: 'Now they are ringing their bells. Soon they will be wringing their hands.'"
D. February 11, 2006. "The Cuban missile crisis, too, came about not because of the Russians' presence there (that was a consequence) but because Kennedy was planning to invade Cuba within a year or so. In the end Kennedy made a compromise (to his credit), something that Bush and his people would not and could not have done."
12 One possible exception may be McKinley against Spain in 1898. Yet he is an exception within an exception. The war against Spain had become popular by 1898; but McKinley was swept into war; he did not choose it to enhance his prestige.
13 D. June 6, 2001. "The Left and Liberals are weak everywhere. They have economic programs, whereas nationalism is not a program: it fills emotional, sentimental, mental, and spiritual needs."
D. May 28, 2005. "Liberalism, as a vital political ideology, is dead, but the Democrats don't know that. They have been, and are, more conservative in foreign policy than are the Republicans. But (a) this does not even occur to them, (b) they cower in fear of not seeming nationalist enough. Sic transit causa rei publicae."
D. April 19, 2003. "The cowardice of the Democrats; like the German Social Democrats on 1 August 1914, or the Catholic Centre Party on 23 March 1933. Not exactly, but largely so."
14 D. February 11, 2002. "Gladstone 1879 about Afghanistan: 'Remember the rights of the savage as we call him. Remember . . . his humble home, remember that the sanctity of life in the hill villages of Afghanistan among the winter snows, is as inviolable in the eyes of Almighty God as can be your own.'"
D. February 14, 2002. "One American killed in combat. Hundreds of Afghans by our 'friendly fire.' This refers to what 'Defense' Secretary Rumsfeld calls 'nothing but collateral damage.' I write about this in a letter to The New York Times. They will not print it."
15 D. February 8, 2002. "The Democrats do not dare criticize Bush's 'Defense' budget. What they ought to say is that it is not for Defense but for Offense."
16 D. April 30, 2003. "Bush, as early as 2001: 'It's great to be commander in chief of this nation.'"
17 D. February 21, 2002. "It seems to me that this diary is more and more like Reck-Malleczewen's Tagebuch eines Verzweifelten. My literary career is such as I had never expected or perhaps even wanted. But I despair of this nation and of many of its people. I think that the 21st century will not be the American century, but that some giant and unprecedented catastrophe may smite this country, probably of its own making, and perpetrated by one or more of their own. (Example: I do not fear an Arab crashing

into the Limerick nuclear towers, but an American in a state of sexual or ideological frenzy.)"

18 D. February 27, 2002. "I read that many of the Enron subsidiaries, 'partnerships,' had names from Star Wars: 'Chewbacca,' 'Jedi,' . . . , etc. Telling this is."

19 D. September 10, 2005. "The dark, very dark corners of American history. CIA operations now are more secret and horrid doings than 'intelligence.' Probably in 1963, too, when it seemed to me that this frenetic fool Oswald had been taken up by the CIA a few months before he shot Kennedy. With that shooting the CIA had nothing to do; but they were frightened by the prospect that Oswald, when arrested and interrogated, would spit out his once CIA connection. Hence getting that gangster Ruby to shoot him next day; and—perhaps—their getting rid of Ruby a year later. Am not sure about this but think it quite plausible."

20 D. October 17, 2001. "War was a profession for a long time—until the mobilization of masses of nationals. Now getting to be a profession again." D. February 6, 2006. "Much of war now: mass killings from a distance. Soldiers' heads full of video games: 'We zap them!' American warplanes now named 'Predators,' 'Raptors.'"

21 D. August 25, 2006. "God will always smite, or chastise, those who think that they are his Chosen People."

22 D. January 20, 2007. "Wendell Berry: 'Rodents and rats live with the laws of supply and demand. Human beings live with the laws of justice and mercy.' Or: they should. How true."

23 One example: what has happened to money. A century ago money was physically solid: its paper certificates exchangeable for gold or silver at par value. Yet for decades now, our money or stocks or bonds are not even on paper or in our actual possessions. They are potential values, consisting of configurations of graphic dust recorded on disks or films, deposited in distant institutions somewhere else. This is explained as part and parcel of the Information Revolution. But the very word information is false. It is not in-formation. Its proper description is the imaging of matter.

24 D. July 8, 2005. "What is 'ownership' now? What are 'assets'? People who are told and who think that they are owners are mere renters."

25 D. April 18, 2003. "Can democracy (as we at least have known it) survive the disappearance of liberalism? May be worth a book."

26 Reagan 1982: America's "divine destiny" is to reaffirm "this nation's special calling." George W. Bush about "Progress," 2002: "America is the hope of all mankind." 2001: "America must fight the enemies of Progress."

27 D. May 19, 2001. "Bush's Secretary of the Treasury: tax cuts will give more money to Americans 'to have bigger houses and bigger cars.' Vice-President Cheney: Conservation is no solution, the solution is to produce more and more 'energy.' These are our Conservatives."

28 D. December 18, 2000. "At night I read the last number of The Catholic Historical Review and I am heartened (in a melancholy way). The standards of this journal are better now than they were, say, forty years ago. . . . Most of its articles and reviews are written by professors in small and obscure and provincial colleges and universities. I should write at least a postcard to some of these struggling men and women to encourage them. Sursum corda."
D. February 11, 2001. "The young conservatives of isi in West Chester. Their minds are more independent than what their adversaries may think. They recognize the shallowness of present 'conservative' politicians and publicists such as Novak or Buckley. Some of them are fairly well-read."
D. May 19, 2005. "Yesterday I went with Ann King to give a talk to the history club in St. Joseph's Prep. The young students gave me an excellent impression, especially Ann's son Leo. Intelligent, quiet, well-mannered, introspective, kind. These young American Catholics may be the salt of the earth."

29 D. April 19, 2003. "People ask me how much fun it is to write. No, I say: the fun is not writing, that is work, the fun (if it is fun at all) is having written. It occurs to me that this is the v. opposite of sex. (A good aphorism perhaps, but not really true in every instance, esp. not for women. The 'finish' in lovemaking means much to me, as in the case of fine wine.)"

30 D. December 6, 2006. Goethe: "Was man in der Jugend begehrt hat, hat man im Alter die Ftille. [What one wished for when young one gets a fill when one is old.] Wise and true—in most circumstances, without people being much aware of it. But 'Ftille' [fulfillment?] in old age is hardly more than contentment. Gissing: 'Contentment so often means resignation, abandonment of the hope seen to be forbidden.' That too is not always so. Acceptance: yes."

31 Do not think that I am against specialists. To the contrary: I respect them; and I am saddened by their gradual disappearance. They have loved their subjects, after all. For the specialist described in the hoary nineteenth-century adage as someone who knows more and more about less and less is, alas, a rare bird nowadays. Instead, we have Experts who know less and less about more and more.

32 D. February 1, 2005. ". . . in the words and thoughts of even those who hate or dislike us there is always at least a small crumb of reality."

33 D. February 8, 2001. "I finish Dava Sobel's truly excellent Galileo book. I did not know that Milton and Hobbes and Elsevir took the trouble to visit Galileo around 1640, two or three years, before he died. This is amazing, this kind of communication among interested people (Milton and Hobbes were not astronomers or scholars, Elsevir a Dutch printer & publisher). They did not flit to Florence in 90 minutes from Heathrow or Amsterdam but they braved the then feared and dangerous—passage of the Alps, among other dreadful wear & tear of traveling in those days.

This too gives the lie to Modern Communications. Galileo was not a Nobel Prize winner, he was not a celebrity, he did not attend conferences, etc. Yet they knew about him and desired to meet him. There are academics and scholars, within thirty miles from here, dozens of them, now who have never even looked at books that I had written in their 'field,' about their 'subjects.' I am not writing this to complain, but to put down what I think of the Information Age and the Communications Revolution—worse than misnomers. Again: the trouble is not with people's inability to think but with their unwillingness to think—i.e., lack of imagination, lack of curiosity. (Four hundred years ago a 'curieux,' in French, meant an intellectual.) I had noticed the same phenomenon reading the correspondence of Vico, who was even less of a Celebrity than Galileo, who taught in Naples, which at the time was a fairly backward university: yet people in faraway France knew about him and corresponded with him."

34 Including myself. At noon every weekday, I walk out to my mailbox on the road. As I gather the accumulation of mail, my heart sinks as I clutch (not without difficulty) the journals and magazines sent to me, to many of which I do not subscribe, and to the daily *New York Times*, to which I do. Sometimes the Saturday delivery of the latter is thickened with the supplements of the Sunday edition: an extra three pounds of paper to carry, but the physical burden of which is nothing compared to the sinking feeling they bring to my mind.

35 As the so-called Industrial Revolution grew to completion, about 130 years ago, for the first time a working man could afford to keep his wife at home. She needed not work outside of it. That lasted, by and large, for less than a century. (As did the Industrial Revolution. In 1874 in England, around 1910 in the United States for the first time, more people were employed in industry than in agriculture. By 1960 in the United States more people were employed in administration and in services than in industrial and agricultural work together.)

36 "The Academy of Music for the Orchestra is gone. The Orchestra now performs in the Kimmel Center, an enormous crimson-painted, airport-like hangar. Sixteen years ago I was in a pastry shop in Helsinki, Finland, full of women and old ladies talking and sipping coffee or tea, before the concert of the Helsinki Philharmonic. What a bourgeois scene in the midst of so-called socialist welfare-state Scandinavia! I felt a sense of permanence, a sense that, say, thirty years later the same kind of people, the same kind of orchestra, the same kind of city life would prevail—when the Philadelphia Orchestra would be performing (if at all) in the King of Prussia Mall."

37 D. April 28, 2006. "Yesterday I drove into Philadelphia, for a radio interview. . . . I got in early, walked over to Rittenhouse Square, which was full of people and still nice. Around me a Philadelphia that I remember but no longer know. The McIlhenny house, '1914,' shut down, its windows sightless, with a gray protective film covering them. The Barclay bar, where I

had so many memories, now must be entered through a door from the street; it is a kind of grill-room."

38 D. December 28, 2006. "Impressionism tells, or should tell us, in retrospect, that it is participation. The 'reality' is not outside but what the painter sees: whence what he can suggest. Of course these painters did not know the historic meaning of this. But their impressionism thus preceded quantum physics by about a half-century. (Of course: the artist is the antenna of the race—or, rather, of civilization.) After that: cubism, abstract art, etc.—and string theory in physics."

D. August 16, 2006. "Impressionism: the great recognition, of course not only of plein-air, but that the world outside us is inseparable from what we see from what comes from inside us, whence we must illustrate ('lustrate,' in the original sense of that word) what and how we see. Thus 'Impressionism' was not a symptom of decadence but a surge of consciousness. . . . The degeneration after it was awful but it will not last."

39 Lathrop: "The finest art, the finest in life, is formed by love." (He disappeared, drowned while repairing his boat on the New England coast during the September 1938 hurricane.) Garber: "I am a very happy man. I am a simple man. . . . I am enthusiastic about my painting. I have few theories about it. . . . I had a wonderful life." (He died at the age of seventy-eight. He had fallen off a ladder.) He "would lovingly touch a small blossom from his garden and growl at his daughter: 'You only have to look at a flower to know there's a God!'" (from the reminiscences of his daughter).

40 D. December 20, 2000. "Tonight the monthly Planning Commission meeting. Blessedly short. (It is very cold tonight.) After the agenda a little superficial banter. . . . Not about essentials: we (they) are more and more dependent on the technical statements of engineers and other experts, whereby essentials are obscured and often not dealt with. This is not democracy at best. But it is also not American democracy at its worst."

41 D. December 19, 2000. "Yesterday I go to the Orphans' Court in West Chester with Ted Ryan and our township attorney for the judge to approve the transfer of the ownership of the Anderson Burial Ground to the township. This is the end of a more than four-year-old process. It goes well and swiftly and I am mildly impressed by the respectful demeanor of the people in the courtroom when Judge Wood comes in."

42 And now our three acres have become an animal refuge, too, for many animals who were driven out of their habitats by the "developments" around us. Besides the habitual squirrels and rabbits and groundhogs we have a herd of deer, two foxes (last winter a coyote), in the air and in the stream all kinds of birds and waterfowl, including herons and a white egret and an occasional stately swan, and a bald eagle appearing once in a while.

43 D. February 28, 2001. ". . . nothing ever occurs in our dreams that we had not experienced or thought or dreamt about before. 'We live forward but we can only think backward' is as applicable to dreams as to thinking

awake. Only the associations are more varied ones. In sum: when we dream we do not really think differently, we only remember differently."

44 D. August 13, 2001. "[Said] De Gaulle. For some people. For me: a leaking ship."

45 My platoon includes my carpenter, my house painter, my plumber, my electrician. We have known each other, we have respected each other, we have depended on each other for many decades now. The president of my bank, the superintendent of my local school district (giant building less than one mile from me demanding more than half of ten thousand dollars from me each year), my representative in the Congress of the United States, I do not know them and they know me not.

46 D. January 18, 2005. "Sixty years ago today, 18 Jan. '45, 9:45 A.M. Budapest, the first Russians. It was something else than 'liberation,' it was Zero Hour. From then on, Russia and America. And now only America, with dwarves ruling it, and the world. I knew what the Russians meant, and I went, fled to America, for an older, more decent, freer life in a free country, in a free world. So much of that now . . . gone."

47 D. May 9, 2002. "Most Americans have no sense or vision that the entire so-called Modern Age is over. Europeans uneasily sense this but have no longer any vigor to resist it."

48 One example. In 1705 the city fathers of Philadelphia outlawed fornication, which was a rather medieval thing to do, and added the clause that the innocent spouses of the guilty parties had the right to sue for divorce, which was very modern, very American.

D. March 8, 2001. "Near Pasadena we drive by a fundamentalist church with a sign outside: 'Dieting for Jesus.'"

49 D. January 28, 2001. "I go to Mass and walk out, during the sermon. The pastor speaks of angels and saints in Heaven watching the Superbowl."

50 D. June 26, 2005. "Didn't go to church and didn't get the Sunday New York Times. Relieved by neglecting the latter but not the former."

51 D. April 22, 2007. "We are living through the spiritualization of matter. That is much of what Catholicism is about: but now, with abstraction rising everywhere, what will the Church do with that?"

52 D. July 15, 2007. "Went to Mass, and took Communion. The Gospel about the Good Samaritan. The priest's sermon was deeply felt, honest. . . . Mary's has now been half-empty, few young people. I do not mind being among a churchgoing people who are a minority. I know this is wrong, but at least think that this is not because I am a snob, it is because of my distrust and even fear of crowds, including energetic crowds of believers."

53 D. January 20, 2002. "The Vatican declared a very fine thing, that Jews and Christians belong together in expecting the Messiah except of course that the former did not recognize His first coming. A good-hearted and wise gesture to Jews."

Bibliography

The Published Writings of John Lukacs, 1947–2012

THIS IS A BIBLIOGRAPHY *of my published writings from 1947 through 2012. It is divided into four parts: books; articles (including essays and pre- and postpublication excerpts from books); reviews (including review-essays); and miscellaneous items, including articles in encyclopedias, verbatim texts of interviews, letters to editors, contributions to symposia and roundtables, and obituaries.*

Helen Lukacs, my granddaughter, assembled the bulk of this bibliography in 2003. This updated bibliography lists all my books published since 2003, but it does not include the considerable number of articles, book reviews, essays, and other miscellaneous writings of mine after that.

John Lukacs
December 2012

Part I: Books

1953

1. *The Great Powers and Eastern Europe.* New York: American Book Company. Bibliography and index.
    a. Reprinted: Chicago: Regnery, 1953.

1959

1. Tocqueville, Alexis de. *"The European Revolution" and Correspondence with Gobineau.* Introduced, edited, and translated by John Lukacs. Garden City, NY: Doubleday. Index.
    a. Reprinted: Gloucester, MA: Peter Smith, 1968.
    b. Reprinted: Westport, CT: Greenwood Press, 1974.

1961

1. *A History of the Cold War.* Garden City, NY: Doubleday. Index.
    a. Paperbound edition: Garden City, NY: Anchor Books, 1962.

b. German edition: *Geschichte des Kalten Krieges*. Gütersloh: Sigbert Mohn Verlag, 1962.
c. French edition: *Guerre Froide*. Paris: Gallimard, 1962.
d. Spanish edition: *Historia de la Guerra Fria*. Mexico City: Herrero, 1962.

1965

1. *Decline and Rise of Europe: A Study in Recent History, with Particular Emphasis on the Development of a European Consciousness*. Garden City, NY: Doubleday. Bibliography and index.
   a. Reprinted: Westport, CT: Greenwood Press, 1976.

1966

1. *A New History of the Cold War*. Extended edition of *A History of the Cold War*, 1961. Garden City, NY: Doubleday Anchor. Index.
   a. German edition: *Konflikte der Weltpolitik nach 1945*. Lausanne: Editions Rencontre, 1970.
   b. German paperbound edition: DTV-Weltgeschichte des 20. Jahrhunderts, Band 12. Munich, 1970.

1968

1. *Historical Consciousness; or, the Remembered Past*. New York: Harper and Row. Idearium and index of names.
   a. Reprinted: New York: Schocken Books, 1985. New and extended edition, with a new introduction and conclusion.
   b. Reprinted: New Brunswick, NJ: Transaction Publishers, 1994. Includes a new introduction by the author and a foreword by Russell Kirk.
   c. Hungarian edition: *A t rt nelmi tudat: avagy a m lt eml kezete*. Budapest: Európa Könyvkiadó.

1970

1. *The Passing of the Modern Age*. New York: Harper and Row. Index.
   a. Paperbound edition: New York: Harper and Row, 1972.
   b. Spanish edition: *El fin de la edad moderna*. Mexico City: Editorial Novaro, S.A., 1975.

c. Japanese edition: *Dai katoki no gendai*. Tokyo: Perikansha, 1978.

1975

1. *A Sketch of the History of Chestnut Hill College, 1924–1974*. Chestnut Hill, PA: Chestnut Hill College. Appendices.

1976

1. *The Last European War: September 1939–December 1941*. Garden City, NY: Anchor Press. Bibliographical remarks, abbreviations, and index.
   a. Reprinted: London: Routledge and Kegan Paul, 1977.
   b. Paperbound edition: New Haven, CT: Yale University Press, 2001.
   c. German edition: *Die Entmachtung Europas. Der letzte europäische Krieg, 1939–1941*. Stuttgart: Klett-Cotta, 1978. (Somewhat abbreviated edition.)
   d. Hungarian edition: *Az európai világháború, 1939–1941*. Budapest: Európa Könyvkiadó, 1995.
   e. Portuguese edition: *Á ultima guerra européia, Septembro 1939–Dezembro 1941*. Rio de Janeiro: Editora Nova Fronteira, 1980.
   f. French edition: *La dernière guerre européenne, Septembre 1939–Décembre 1941*. Paris: Fayard, 1977.

1978

1. *1945: Year Zero*. Garden City, NY: Doubleday. Index.
   a. Hungarian edition: *1945, a nulla év*. Budapest: Európa Könyvkiadó, 1996. Includes a special appendix for this edition.

1981

1. *Philadelphia: Patricians and Philistines, 1900–1950*. New York: Farrar, Straus and Giroux, 1981. Bibliography and index.
   a. Paperbound edition: Philadelphia: Institute for the Study of Human Issues, 1982.

1984

1. *Outgrowing Democracy: A History of the United States in the Twentieth Century*. Garden City, NY: Doubleday. Index.
   a. Paperbound edition: Lanham, MD: University Press of America, 1986.
   b. Hungarian edition: *Az Egyesült Államok 20. századi története*. Budapest: Gondolat, 1988. Also: Budapest: Európa Könyvkiadó, 2002. Includes a new appendix.

1986

1. *Immigration and Migration: A Historical Perspective*. AICF Monograph Series, paper no. 5. Monterey, VA: American Immigration Control Foundation.

1988

1. *Budapest 1900: A Historical Portrait of a City and Its Culture*. New York: Weidenfeld and Nicolson. Bibliography and index.
   a. Paperbound edition: New York: Grove Press, 1990.
   b. Japanese edition: *Budapesuto no seikimatsu: toshi to bunka no rekishiteki shozo*. Tokyo: Hakusuisha, 1991.
   c. French edition: *Budapest 1900: portrait historique d'une ville et de sa culture*. Paris: Quai Voltaire, 1990.
   d. German edition: *Ungarn in Europa: Budapest um die Jahrhundertwende*. Berlin: Siedler, 1990. Includes "Vorwort zur deutschen Ausgabe," a special foreword for this edition.
   e. Hungarian edition: *Budapest 1900: A város és kultúrája*. Budapest: Európa Könyvkiadó, 1991. Also bilingual edition: Budapest: Európa Könyvkiadó, 2003.

1990

1. *Confessions of an Original Sinner*. New York: Ticknor and Fields.
   a. Reprinted: South Bend, IN: St. Augustine's Press, 2000.
   b. Hungarian edition: *Egy eredendö bûnös vallomásai*. Budapest: Európa Könyvkiadó, 2001.

1991

1. *The Duel: 10 May–31 July 1940: The Eighty-Day Struggle between Churchill and Hitler.* New York: Ticknor and Fields. References, abbreviations, bibliographical essay, and index.
   a. British edition: *The Duel: Hitler vs. Churchill: 10 May–31 July 1940.* Oxford: Oxford University Press, 1992.
   b. Paperbound editions: New York: Ticknor and Fields, 1991. Also: Oxford: Oxford University Press, 1992. Also: New Haven, CT: Yale University Press, 2001.
   c. Danish edition: *Duellen.* Copenhagen: Fremad, 1991.
   d. German edition: *Churchill und Hitler: Der Zweikampf: 10. Mai–31. Juli 1940.* Stuttgart: Deutsche Verlags-Anstalt, 1992.
   e. French edition: *Le Duel Churchill/Hitler.* Paris: Laffont, 1992.
   f. Dutch edition: *De Krachtmeting 10 Mei–31 Juli.* Amsterdam: Uitgeverij Contact, 1992.
   g. Italian edition: *Il Duello.* Milan: Longanesi, 1991. Also: *Il Duello 10 maggio–31 luglio 1940: ottanta giorni decisivi della storia del nostro secolo.* Milan: TEA/Longanesi, 1995.
   h. Hungarian edition: *A párviadal.* Budapest: Európa Könyvkiadó, 1993. Includes a special appendix for this edition.
   i. Swedish edition: *Duellen: Kempen mellan Churchill och Hitler 10 Maj–31 Juli 1940.* Stockholm: Tidens Förlag, 1994.
   j. Hebrew edition: *ha-Du-kerav: shemonim yeme hitmodedut ben Ts'erts'il le-Hitler, 10 be-Mai-31 be-Yuli 1940.* Tel Aviv: Misrad ha-bitahon, 1994.
   k. Japanese edition: *Hitora tai chachiru: hachijunichikan no gekito.* Tokyo: Kyodo Tsushinsha, 1995.
   l. British paperbound edition: *The Duel: Hitler vs. Churchill, 10 May–31 July 1940.* London: Phoenix Press, 2000.
   m. Swedish paperbound edition: *Duellen: Kempen mellan Churchill och Hitler 10 Maj–31 Juli 1940.* Stockholm: Raben Prisma, 2002.
   n. Portuguese edition: *O Duelo.* Rio de Janeiro: Jorge Zahar, 2002.

1993

1. *The End of the Twentieth Century and the End of the Modern Age.* New York: Ticknor and Fields.
    a. Dutch edition: *Het ende van de moderne tijd.* Amsterdam and Antwerp: Uitgverij, 1993.
    b. Turkish edition: *Yirminci yüzyilin ve modern çagin sonu.* Istanbul: Sabah Kitaplari, 1993.
    c. Hungarian edition: *A XX. század és az újkor vége.* Budapest: Európa Könyvkiadó, 1994, 436. Also: Budapest: Európa Könyvkiadó, 2000. 2nd ed.
    d. Bulgarian edition: Sofia: Obsidian, 1994.
    e. German edition: *Die Geschichte geht weiter: Das Ende des 20. Jahrhunderts und die Wiederkehr des Nationalismus.* Munich: List, 1994.
    f. Portuguese edition: *O Fim do Século 20 e o fim da era moderna.* Sao Paulo: Editora Nova Cultura, 1995.
    g. Swedish edition: *Slutet på det tjugonde århundradet och den moderna tidens slut.* Stockholm: Raben Prisma, 1998.

1994

1. *Destinations Past: Traveling through History with John Lukacs.* Columbia, MO: University of Missouri Press.
    a. Hungarian edition: *Visszafelé . . . Utazások 1954–1996.* Budapest: Európa Könyvkiadó, 2001.

1997

1. *The Hitler of History.* New York: Alfred A. Knopf. Bibliography, abbreviations, and index.
    a. German edition: *Hitler: Geschichte und Geschichtsschreibung.* Munich: Luchterhand, 1997.
    b. Paperbound edition: New York: Vintage, 1998.
    c. Italian edition: *Dossier Hitler.* Milan: Longanesi, 1998.
    d. Portuguese edition: *O Hitler da história.* Rio de Janeiro: Jorge Zahar, 1998.
    e. Hungarian edition: *A történelmi Hitler.* Budapest: Európa Könyvkiadó, 1998.
    f. Swedish edition: *Hitler i historien.* Stockholm: Prisma, 1999.

g. Dutch edition: *Hitler en de geschiedenis. Hitler's plaats in de 20ste eeuw.* Antwerp/Amsterdam: Carus/Anthos, 1999.
h. German paperbound edition: *Hitler: Geschichte und Geschichtsschreibung.* Berlin: Ullstein-Propyläen Taschenbuch, 1999.
i. Italian paperbound edition: *Dossier Hitler.* Milan: TEA/ Longanesi, 2000.
j. British edition: *The Hitler of History: Hitler's Biographers on Trial.* London: Weidenfeld and Nicolson, 2000.
k. Extended Dutch edition, 2008.

2. *George F. Kennan and the Origins of Containment, 1944–1946: The Kennan-Lukacs Correspondence.* Introduction by John Lukacs. Columbia, MO: University of Missouri Press. Bibliography and index.
    a. Paperbound edition: Columbia, MO: University of Missouri Press, 1992.

1998

1. *A Thread of Years.* New Haven, CT: Yale University Press.
    a. Paperbound edition: New Haven, CT: Yale University Press, 1998.
    b. Hungarian edition: *Évek.* Budapest: Európa Könyvkiadó, 1999.

1999

1. *Five Days in London, May 1940.* New Haven, CT: Yale University Press. Bibliography and index.
    a. Hungarian edition: *Öt nap Londonban: 1940 május.* Budapest: Európa Könyvkiadó, 2000.
    b. German edition: *Fünf Tage in London: England und Deutschland in May 1940.* Berlin: Siedler, 2000.
    c. Swedish edition: *Churchills Ödesstund: Fem Dagar I London, maj 1940.* Stockholm: Prisma, 2001.
    d. Portuguese edition: *Cinco Dias em Londres: negociações que mudaram o rumo da II Guerra.* Rio de Janeiro: Jorge Zahar, 2001.
    e. Italian edition: *Cinque Giorno a Londra, Maggio 1940.* London: Carbaccio, 2001.

   f. Korean edition: Seoul: Jungsim Publishing, 2001.
   g. Paperbound edition: New Haven, CT: Yale University Press, 2001.
   h. Australian edition: *Five Days in London, May 1940.* Carlton, VIC: Scribe Publications, 2001.
   i. French edition: *Churchill: Londres, Mai 1940.* Paris: Odile Jacob, 2002.
   j. Spanish edition: *Cinco dias in Londres: Mayo de 1940.* Madrid: Turner, 2001.
   k. British folio editions, 2011, 2012.

2000

1. *A Student's Guide to the Study of History.* Wilmington, DE: ISI Books.

2002

1. *At the End of an Age.* New Haven, CT: Yale University Press.
   a. Danish edition, 2002.
   b. Portuguese edition, 2002.
   c. Russian edition, 2003.
   d. Hungarian edition, 2003.
   e. Czech edition, 2009.
2. *Churchill: Visionary. Statesman. Historian.* New Haven, CT: Yale University Press.
   a. Portuguese edition: *Churchill: Visionario, Estadista, Historiador.* Rio de Janeiro: Jorge Zahar, 2003.
   b. Hebrew edition: Tel Aviv, 2003. Translated by Arie Hashavia.
   c. Hungarian edition, 2003.
   d. Swedish edition, 2004.
   e. Latvian edition, 2009.
   f. Italian edition, 2009.

2004

1. *A New Republic.* Extended edition of *Outgrowing Democracy: A History of the United States in the Twentieth Century,* 1984. New Haven, CT: Yale University Press.
   a. Portuguese edition, 2004.
   b. Hungarian edition, 2005.

2005

1. *Democracy and Populism: Fear and Hatred.* New Haven, CT: Yale University Press.
    a. Hungarian edition, 2006.
    b. Slovak edition, 2006.
    c. Italian edition, 2007.
2. *Remembered Past: John Lukacs on History, Historians, and Historical Knowledge—A Reader.* Edited by Mark G. Malvasi and Jeffrey O. Nelson. Wilmington, DE: ISI Books.

2006

1. *June 1941: Hitler and Stalin.* New Haven, CT: Yale University Press.
    a. Czech edition, 2006.
    b. Hungarian edition, 2006.
    c. Korean edition, 2006.
    d. Italian edition, 2006.
    e. Latvian edition, 2007.
    f. Estonian edition, 2007.
    g. Polish edition, 2007.
    h. Swedish edition, 2007.
    i. Portuguese edition, 2007.
    j. Mexican (Spanish) edition, 2008.
    k. Spanish edition (Madrid), 2007.

2007

1. *George Kennan: A Study of Character.* New Haven, CT: Yale University Press.

2008

1. *Blood, Toil, Tears, and Sweat: The Dire Warning—Churchill's First Speech as Prime Minister.* New York: Basic Books.
    a. Spanish edition, 2008.
    b. Portuguese edition, 2008.

2009

1. *Last Rites*. New Haven, CT: Yale University Press.
    a. Hungarian edition, 2009.
2. *American Austen: The Forgotten Writings of Agnes Repplier.* Edited and introduced by John Lukacs. Wilmington, DE: ISI Books.

2010

1. *The Legacy of the Second World War.* New Haven, CT: Yale University Press.
    a. Dutch edition, 2008.
    b. Hungarian edition, 2010.
    c. French edition, 2011.
2. *Through the History of the Cold War: The Kennan-Lukacs Correspondence*. Philadelphia: University of Pennsylvania Press.
    a. Hungarian edition, 2010.

2011

1. *The Future of History*. New Haven, CT: Yale University Press.
    a. Hungarian edition, 2011.

Part II: Articles

1947

1. "Communist Tactics in Balkan Government." *Thought*, June: 219–44.

1949

1. "Political Expediency and Soviet Russian Military Operations." *Journal of Central European Affairs* (January): 390–411.
2. "A Hungarian Traveler in Pennsylvania, 1831." *Pennsylvania Magazine of History and Biography*, January: 64–75.

1950

1. "The Inter-Service Dispute Viewed with European Eyes." *U.S. Naval Institute Proceedings* (November): 1237–47.

1951

1. "The Resurgent Fascists." *Current History* (April): 213–18.

2. "The Story behind Hitler's Greatest Blunder." *New York Times Magazine*, June 17: 10ff.

1952

1. "The Policy of Containment" (Part 1). *Commonweal*, August 29: 503–6.
2. "Diplomacy in a Vacuum: The Policy of Containment" (Part 2). *Commonweal*, September 5: 530–32.
3. "Foreign Policy: The Confusion of Ideology." *Catholic World*, December: 195–201.
4. "The Last Days of the Ritz." *Commonweal*, December 5: 219–22.
5. "The Winning Side." *Freeman*, December 29: 242.

1953

1. "On Literary Correspondence." *Commonweal*, February 20: 500–504.

1954

1. "The Totalitarian Temptation." *Commonweal*, January 22: 394–99.
    a. Reprinted (abridged) in *Commonweal Confronts the Century*, edited by Patrick Jordan and Paul Baumann, 56–62. New York: Simon & Schuster, 1999.
2. "The Return of A. Pruett Ripperger." *Commonweal*, May 28: 202–3.
3. "The Crusaders." *Commonweal* (under the pseudonym "Tacitulus"), June 18: 263–66.
4. "Russian Armies in Western Europe: 1799, 1814, 1917." *American Slavic and East European Review* (October): 319–37.

1955

1. "The Meaning of Naval Prestige." *U.S Naval Institute Proceedings* (December): 1351–60.

1956

1. "New India and 'Age-Old Christianity.'" *Medical Missionary*, May/June: 67–70.

1957

1. "On Public and Popular Opinion." *Anchor Review*: 221–40.
2. "Lessons of the Hungarian Revolution." *Commentary*, September: 223–30.
    a. Pursuant correspondence: December: 188.

1958

1. "Intellectuals, Catholics and the Intellectual Life." *Modern Age* (Winter 1957–58): 40–53.
2. "The World's Cities—Philadelphia." *Encounter*, February: 34–41.
    a. Reprinted in *English: Selected Readings*, vol. 1. University of Chicago, Syllabus Division, University of Chicago Press, September: 257–70.
3. "Was Fascism an Episode?" *Commonweal*, March 14: 606–9.
4. "Dwight Macdonald: Another Orwell?" *America* (under the pseudonym "Orville Williams"), May 17: 224–27.
5. "Conversation in Vienna." *Commonweal*, August 8: 466–67.
6. "The Death of Hard News." *Encounter*, September: 72–73.

1959

1. "De Tocqueville Centenary." *French Historical Studies* 1: 250–51.
2. "The American Imperial Disease." *American Scholar* (Spring): 141–50.
    a. Pursuant correspondence: *American Scholar* (Summer): 402–8; (Autumn): 540–41.
    b. Reprinted in *Executive* (Harvard University Graduate School of Business Administration) (May): 16, 21.
    c. Reprinted in *The Challenge of Politics: Ideas and Issues*, edited by Alvin Z. Rubinstein and Garold W. Thumm, 392–97. Englewood Cliffs, NJ: Prentice-Hall, 1965.
3. "Letter to England: A Second Holland Is Not Enough." *Encounter*, May: 59–62.
4. "Ten Misconceptions of Anti-Communism." *United States Naval Institute Proceedings* (May): 64–69.
    a. Summary and excerpts in *Commonweal*, May 29: 227.
    b. Reprinted in *An American Foreign Policy Reader*, edited by Harry Howe Ransom, 635–42. New York: Thomas Y. Crowell, 1965.

5. "De Tocqueville's Message for America." *American Heritage*, June: 99–102.

1960

1. "Intellectual Class or Intellectual Profession?" In *Intellectuals*, edited by George B. de Huszar, 517–23. Glencoe, IL: Free Press.
2. "The Grand Mountain Hotel." *Harper's Bazaar*, May: 210.

1961

1. "What 'Moonlighting' Reveals: Certain Problems of American College Teachers." *University Bookman* (Summer): 86–90.
2. "Bancroft: The Historian as Celebrity." *American Heritage*, October: 65–68.
    a. Reprinted in *A Sense of History: The Best Writing from the Pages of* American Heritage, with an introduction by Byron Dobell, 410–17. New York: American Heritage Press, 1985.

1962

1. "Poland's Place in the European State System." *Polish Review*, vol. 7, no. 1:47–58.
2. "The Sense of the Past." In *Chester County Day*. Annual newspaper of the Chester County Day Committee of the Women's Auxiliary to the Chester County Hospital (Chester County, PA), October: 6.
3. "Les origins de la guerre froide: le problème historiographique." *Comprendre* (Société Européenne de Culture, Venice) vol. 25: 17–24.

1963

1. "Poker and the American Character." *Horizon*, November: 56–62.
    a. Reprinted in *Philadelphia Inquirer*, March 1, 1964, Today's World section, 6.
    b. Reprinted in *Horizon Bedside Reader*, edited by Charles L. Mee Jr., 252–67. New York: American Heritage Press, 1970.

1964

1. "The Last Days of Alexis de Tocqueville." *Catholic Historical Review* (July): 155–70.
    a. Translated into Hungarian as "Alexis de Tocqueville utolsó napjai." *Vigilia* (Budapest) no. 10 (2002): 739–47.
2. "The Roots of the Dilemma." *Continuum* (Summer): 183–92.

1965

1. "Internationalism and the Nations of Europe." *Worldview*, March: 5–8.
2. "De l'idée d'Europe—son evolution historique." *Revue des sciences politiques* (Toulouse) (June): 349–60.
    a. Excerpted in *Current*, May: 26–37.
3. "The Battle That Began a 100-Year Peace." *New York Times Magazine*, June 13: 10–13.
    a. Excerpted in *New York Times International Edition*, June 18.
4. "Magyar Wedding, Irish Funeral." *Esquire*, August: 34–39.
5. "A magyar nemzet és az európai öntudat." *Irodalmi Ujság*, October 1.

1966

1. "It's Halfway to 1984." *New York Times Magazine*, January 2: 8ff.
    a. Reprinted in *A Complete Course in Freshman English*, edited by Harry Shaw, 761–68. New York: Harper & Row, 1967.
    b. Reprinted in *The Odyssey Reader: Ideas and Style*, edited by Newman P. Birk and Genevieve B. Birk, 59–68. New York: Odyssey Publishing, 1968.
    c. Reprinted in *The Lively Rhetoric*, edited by Alexander Scharbach and Ralph H. Singleton, 159–68. New York: Holt, Rinehart and Winston, 1968.
    d. Reprinted in *Perspectives on Our Time*, edited by Francis X. Davy and Robert E. Burkhart, 177–85. New York: Houghton Mifflin, 1970.
    e. Reprinted in *The Experience of Writing*, edited by William D. Baker and T. Benson Strandness, 189–92. Englewood Cliffs, NJ: Prentice Hall, 1970.

f. Reprinted in *Insight: A Rhetoric Reader*, edited by Emil Burtik, 61–70. New York: Lippincott, 1970.

2. "The Changing Face of Progress." *Texas Quarterly* (Winter): 7–14.

1967

1. Excerpt from *A History of the Cold War*. In *Great Issues in Western Civilization*, vol. 2., edited by Brian Tierney, Donald Kagan, and L. Pearce Williams, 669–78. New York: Random House.
2. "Magyar széljegyzetek." *Irodalmi Ujság*, August 1: 3.
3. "A Dissenting View of the Day That Shook the World." *New York Times Magazine*, October 22: 32ff.
    a. Pursuant correspondence: January 7, 1968: 112–13.

1968

1. "How Ideas Move: Notes for a Future Historian of 'Revisionism.'" *Worldview*, July/August: 6–9. (Mangled by editors.)
2. "Speaking of Books: Historians and Novelists." *New York Times Magazine*, February 25: 2ff.
3. "The Changing Campus." *Grackle*, Spring: 16–18.
4. "Elkerülhetö volt—e Magyarország orosz megszállása 1944 ben?" *Irodalmi Ujság*, April 1: 1–16.
5. "Magyar széljegyzetek." *Irodalmi Ujság*, August 1: 5.
6. "America's Malady Is Not Violence, but Savagery." *Commonweal*, November 15: 241–45.
    a. Reprinted in *Violence in America: A Historical and Contemporary Reader*, edited by Thomas Rose, 349–58. New York: Vintage Books.

1969

1. "American Expansion" and "The Great Historical Movements of Our Times." Excerpts from *A History of the Cold War* in *Aspects de la civilization américaine*, edited by Jean Guiget, 271–77. Paris: Libraire Armand Colin, 1969.
2. "The Night Stalin and Churchill Divided Europe." *New York Times Magazine*, October 5: 36–50.
    a. Reprinted in *Richmond Times-Dispatch*, October 5, 1970.

3. "The Paradox of Prosperity." Excerpt from *The Passing of the Modern Age*. *Commentary*, February: 64–69.
    a. Translated into Italian as "Il paradosso della prosperità." *Mercurio* (Rome), November: 7–11.
4. "The Heritage of Yalta." *ACEN News*, July/August: 6–9.
5. "Emancipation or Degradation?" Excerpt from *The Passing of the Modern Age*. *National Review*, August 11: 833–35.
6. "The Bourgeois Interior." Excerpt from *The Passing of the Modern Age*. *American Scholar* (Autumn): 616–40.
    a. Reprinted in *Dialogue*, no. 1: 89–96.
7. "The Transmission of Life: Certain Generalizations about the Demography of Europe's Nations in 1939–1941." *Comparative Studies in Society and History*, October: 442–51.

1971

1. "America May Be in the Last Phase of Its Adolescence." *New York Times Magazine*, December 5: 58–60.

1972

1. "Pornography and the Death Wish." *Triumph*, January: 11–14.
    a. Reprinted in *The Spirit of* Triumph, *1966–1976*, by the Society for the Christian Commonwealth, 45–47.
2. "The End of the Cold War (and Other Clichés)." *Worldview*, February: 5–8.
3. "Rêveuse Bourgeoisie: The Vitality of the European Bourgeoisie during the Decisive Phase of World War II." *Societas: A Review of Social History* (Autumn): 291–306.

1973

1. "The Origins of the Cold War." Excerpts from *A New History of the Cold War*, in *From Metternich to the Beatles: Readings in Modern European History*, edited by Richard C. Lukas, 196–205. New York: New American Library.
2. "'Right and Left,' in America, That Is." *Art International*, January: 81–84.
3. "Bare Ruined Choirs." *Triumph*, April: 22–24.

1974

1. "Wilson Is Overtaking Lenin." *National Review*, February 15: 199–203.
2. "A German Inheritance." *Triumph*, June: 32–34.

1975

1. "The Kirovogard Mystery." *National Review*, January 31: 106–8.
2. "So What Else Is New?" *New York Times Magazine*, February 9: 38ff.
    a. Pursuant correspondence: March 9: 4.
3. "Thirty Years since World War II." *Louisville Courier-Journal and Times*, March 23: 8–13.
4. "The College Is Now a Grandma." *Philadelphia Sunday Bulletin*, June 22, Discovery section, 4–5.
5. "What Solzhenitsyn Means." *Commonweal*, August 1: 296–301.
    a. Pursuant correspondence: October 10: 475–79.
6. "The Postwar World." *New Republic*, August 29: 18–21.
7. "Doctorowurlitzer, or History in Ragtime." *Salmagundi* (Fall 1975–Winter 1976): 285–95.

1976

1. "FDR: The American as Idealistic Pragmatist." Excerpt from *Year Zero. Four Quarters* (Summer): 31–46.

1977

1. "Sans Caviare." *National Review*, April 15: 450–52.

1978

1. "What If? Had Hitler Won the Second World War." In *The People's Almanac # 2*, edited by David Wallechinsky and Irving Wallace, 394–97. New York: Bantam Books.
2. "The Historiographical Problem of Belief and Believers: Religious History in the Democratic Age." Presidential address of the American Catholic Historical Association, 1977. *Catholic Historical Review* (April): 153–67.
3. "Slouching toward Byzantium." *National Review*, April 28: 539–41.

4. "Power and the Twentieth Century." *American Spectator*, June/July: 13–15.
5. "Big Grizzly." (Version of Boies Penrose chapter in *Philadelphia: Patricians and Philistines: 1900–1950.*) *American Heritage*, October/November: 72–81.
6. "A nemzeti becsület védöje: Lukács János történész visszaemlékezére Auer Pálra." *Magyar Hiradó* (Vienna), October 1.

1979

1. "The Continental Express." *National Review*, March 2: 311–13.
2. "What Is Happening to History?" *University Bookman* (Spring): 51–58.
3. "Three Days in London." *American Spectator*, August: 7–14.
4. "The Light from the East" *National Review*, October 26: 1352–60.
    a. Reprinted (abridged) in *The Joys of* National Review, *1955–1980*, edited by Priscilla Buckley, 228–30. New York: National Review Books.
5. "The Monstrosity of Government." Excerpt from *The Passing of the Modern Age*. In *The Politicization of Society*, edited by Kenneth S. Templeton Jr., 391–408. Indianapolis: Liberty Press.

1980

1. "The Tolstoy Locomotive on the Berlin Track." *University Bookman* (Summer): 75–83.
2. "Old World to New," *Salmagundi* (Fall 1980–Winter 1981):105–14. See also Lukacs's remarks in panel discussion, 116–17, 136–37.
3. "American History? American History," *Salmagundi* (Fall 1980–Winter 1981): 172–80. See also Lukacs's remarks in panel discussion, 185–86, 189–92.
4. "The Light in the East." *New Republic*, September 20: 17–19.
    a. Reprinted in *Criticón* (Bonn), November/December.
    b. Reprinted in *La Prensa* (Buenos Aires), March 1, 1981.
    c. Reprinted in *Western Civilization*, vol. 2, edited by William Hughes, 189–93. Guilford, CT: Duskin Publishing Group, 1983.
5. "Obsolete Historians." *Harper's*, November: 80–84.
6. "Polish Omens." *New Republic*, November 29: 14–17.

1981

1. "From Camelot to Abilene." *American Heritage*, February/March: 52–57
2. "Poland: A Lesson of Eastern Europe for the Soviets: Symptomatic of Coming Decline, Hungarian-Born Historian Says." *Pittsburgh Post-Gazette*, March 11: 1–6. Also see insert: "A Very Quotable Historian."
3. "Kovács Imre 1913–1980. Kivételes férfi." *Uj Látóhatá* (Munich), March 30: 425–27.
    a. Translated into Spanish as "El Triunfol de Evelyn Waugh." Suplemento cultural de *La Nueva Provincia* (Bahia Blanca, Argentina), April: 1–6.
4. "Easter in Warsaw." *National Review*, June 12: 658–65.
5. "Agnes Repplier," Part I. *New American Review* (Fall): 13–21.
6. "L'Urss, una pianeta senza più satelliti." *Il Giorno* (Milan), October 6: 7
7. "Uno storico di origini magiare rivisita l'Ungheria. Tremi il potente Cremlino: E rinato l'amor di patria." *Il Sabato* (Milan), October 24–30: 21–22.
8. "Bracing Praise." Excerpt from *Philadelphia 1900–1950. National Review*, December 11: 1450.

1982

1. "In Darkest Transylvania." *New Republic*, February 3: 15–21.
    a. Translated into Hungarian as "Erdély. Európa legszebb és legsötétebb része." *Délamerikai Magyar Hirlap* (Buenos Aires), May.
2. "Open Your Eyes, for God's Sake!" *National Review*, March 5: 223–30.
3. "Alexis de Tocqueville: A Historical Appreciation." *Literature of Liberty* (Spring): 7–34.
4. "Agnes Repplier," Part II. *New American Review* (Spring/Summer): 30–36.
5. "Hitler Becomes a Man." *American Scholar* (Summer): 391–95.
6. "Schuylkill Retains Its Rural Character." *Evening Phoenix* (Phoenixville, PA), October 4, sec. A.
7. "Progress, Our Least Important Product." *Philadelphia Inquirer Magazine*, October 24, Today section, 18ff.

1983

1. "When Hitler Came. Fifty Years Ago." *American Spectator*, May: 11–13.
2. "Happy Birthday, Benito." *American Spectator*, August: 13–17.
3. "A Foreigner in Philadelphia." Excerpt from *Confessions of an Original Sinner*. *Philadelphia*, November: 91–103.

1984

1. "The American Conservatives." *Harper's*, January: 44–49.
    a. Excerpts translated into Hungarian in *Külföldi folyòiratokból*, 116–18.
2. "Two-Faced Germany." *American Spectator*, July: 21–23.

1985

1. "Alexis de Tocqueville" and "Jacob Burckhardt." In *European Writers: The Romantic Century*, vol. 6, edited by Jacques Barzun, 893–912, 1225–44. New York: Charles Scribner's Sons.
2. "American Pacifism—A Historical Perspective." In *Die Kampagne gegen den NATO-Doppellbeschluss*, edited by Gunther Wagenlehner, 70–83. Koblenz: Bernard and Graefe.
3. "Történetirás és regényirás: a mult étvágya és ize." *Történelmi Szemle*, no. 2: 280–88.
    a. Reprinted in *Korunk* (Cluj), January 1999: 44–55.
4. "Remembering Yalta: What Happened and What Did Not." *Harper's*, March: 75–76.
    a. Translations published in many periodicals, including: *V.I.P. Weekly* (Madras), June 17; *Srinitgar Bulletin*, June 18; *Ourvi-Zilly* (Buesti), June 4; *Srinagar*, June 9; *El Heraldo de Mexico*, May 13; *La Estrella de Panama*, May 27; *Swatantra-Gbharat*, May 14; *Gaumi-Hamdard*, May 15; *Kausar*, April 30; *El Diario* (La Paz), May 5.
5. "The Gotthard Walk." *New Yorker*, December 23: 57–77.

1986

1. "A Night at the Dresden Opera." *New Yorker*, March 17: 95–100.
2. "The Lampedusa Mystery." *New York Times*, May 7: sec. A, 31.

3. Excerpts from *Philadelphia: Patricians and Philistines, 1900–1950.* In The Scene, by Clark DeLeon. *Philadelphia Inquirer,* 31 August: sec. B, 2.
4. "The Soviet State at Age 65." *Foreign Affairs* (Fall): 21–36.
    a. Excerpt in *World Peace Report*, December: 2–3.
5. "The Dangerous Summer of 1940." *American Heritage*, October/November: 22–31.
    a. Reprinted in *World History*, vol. 2., by David McComb, 146–50. Guilford, CT: Dushkin Publishing Group, 1990.
6. "The Displaced Persons." *World and I*, November: 675–82.
7. "Après Ski." *National Review*, November 7: 57–59.
8. "The Sound of a Cello." *New Yorker,* December 1: 43–60.
    a. Excerpt translated into Hungarian as "Egy cselló hangja." *Valóság*, no. 5, 1987: 124–25.
    b. Excerpt translated into Hungarian as "A gordonka hangja." *Mozgó Világ*, no. 7, 1987: 674–75.
    c. Excerpt in *In Quest of the Miracle Stag: The Poetry of Hungary*, edited by Ádám Makkai. Chicago: Atlantis-Centaur, 1996.

1987

1. "Heisenberg's Recognitions: The End of the Scientific World View." Excerpt from *Historical Consciousness*. In *Science and Culture in the Western Tradition*, edited by John G. Burke, 257–61. Scottsdale, AZ: Gorsuch Scarisbrick Publishers.
2. "America in the 1980s: Under the Sway of 'Conservative' Constantinism." *New Oxford Review*, April: 7–11.
3. "Unexpected Philadelphia." *American Heritage*, May/June: 72–81.
4. "The Constitution: Could It Be Written Today?" *Philadelphia Inquirer Magazine*, July 5: 101–15.
5. "The Evolving Relationship of History and Sociology." *International Journal of Politics, Culture, and Society* (Fall): 70–88.
    a. Abstracted in *Sociological Abstracts*, October 1988: 1261.
6. "Philadelphia." *TWA Ambassador,* August: 18ff.
7. "Im Schatten von gestern." *Frankfurter Allgemeine Zeitung*, August 29.
8. "Soviets Aren't the Point of Conflict: While We Curse the Old Foe, Threats from the Third World Grow." *Los Angeles Times*, October 2: 7.

9. "Casablanca Revisited." *Four Quarters* (Winter): 35–38.
10. "The Alps." *TWA Ambassador*, November: 32–41.

1988

1. "U.S. Policy towards Eastern Europe: Past, Present, and Future." In *The Uncertain Future: Gorbachev's Eastern Bloc*, edited by Nicholas N. Kittrie and Iván Völgyes, 203–14. New York: Paragon House.
2. "The Riviera in Winter: Menton Then and Now." *Gourmet*, January: 58–61.
    a. Reprinted in *Provence: An Inspired Anthology and Travel Resource*, edited by Barrie Kerper, 262–68. New York: Random House, 2001.
3. "Afghanistan Was Misread by Both Sides." *Los Angeles Times*, February 15: 7.
4. "Budapest 1900: Colors, Words, Sounds." Excerpt from *Budapest 1900*. *American Scholar* (Spring): 253–61.
5. "Budapest in 1900: City and People." Excerpt from *Budapest 1900*. *Hungarian Studies* (April 1): 65–92.
6. "The Reagan Administration—Bitter Afterthoughts." *World and I*, April: 581–87.
7. "A Muscle-Bound America Truly Has Few Options to Chase Bad Guys Away." *Los Angeles Times*, 15 April: 7. (Titles of articles such as these are seldom the choice of the author.)
8. "Nationalism, Not Communism, Is Today's Threat." *Los Angeles Times*, July 4: 6.
9. "Tom Wolfe's Novel and Its Reception as a Significant Historical Event." *New Oxford Review*, September: 6–12.
10. "Corrupt and Diminished, the Communist Party Has Finally Met Its Match." *Los Angeles Times*, October 18: 7.
11. "American Manners." *Chronicles*, November: 9–15.
12. "Budapest in Love and War." Excerpt from *Confessions of an Original Sinner*. *Harper's*, November: 72ff.

1989

1. "America's True Power." *American Heritage*, March: 74–79.
2. "The Rhine." *TWA Ambassador*, July: 38ff.
3. "The Coming of the Second World War." *Foreign Affairs* (Autumn): 165–74.

a. Reprinted (abridged) in *World History*, vol. 2, edited by David McComb, 146–50. Guilford, CT: Dushkin Publishing, 1993.

4. "The Conspiratorial World View of Whittaker Chambers." *New Oxford Review*, November: 5–8.
5. "Let History Be Our Guide." *Los Angeles Times*, November 18.
6. "Hungary in 1938." *New Hungarian Quarterly* (Winter): 46–51.
7. Excerpt from *Budapest 1900. Világosság*, December: 910–21.

1990

1. "Resistance: Simone Weil." *Salmagundi* (Winter/Spring): 106–18.
2. "Hannah Arendt's Intellectual Opportunism." *New Oxford Review*, April: 18–22.
    a. Translated into Hungarian as "Totalitarizmus és érelmeszedés." *Magyar Nemzet*, September 7, 1996.
3. "A Valley's Voyage through Time." *Four Quarters* (Spring): 9–15.
4. "Eastern Europe." Excerpt from *Confessions of an Original Sinner. Wilson Quarterly* (Spring): 37–47.
5. "Born Again Budapest." *Condé Nast Traveler*, April: 140–49.
6. "Der achtzigtägige Zweikampf." *Frankfurter Allgemeine Zeitgung*, May 5.
7. "Scared by Reds, Mugged by Thugs." *Los Angeles Times*, May 21, sec. B, 7.
8. "The Stirrings of History." *Harper's*, August: 41–48.
9. "Letters and Physics, or the Race to the Swiftest." *Salmagundi* (Winter/Spring): 195–96.
10. "Fifty Years Ago: The Eighty-Day Duel." Excerpt from *The Duel. New Hungarian Quarterly* (Autumn): 7ff.
11. "A Professor among Politicians." *Philadelphia*, September: 59–67.
12. "A burzsoá enteriör." Hungarian translation of "The Bourgeois Interior." *Világosság*, October: 739–47.
13. "Connecting with Eastern Europe." *American Heritage*, November: 47–58.
14. "Die Schweiz als Vorbild. Europasymbol und Europagedanke." *Frankfurter Allgemeine Zeitung*, December 15.

1991

1. "Polite Letters and Clio's Fashions." Address at the Irish Conference of Historians, Trinity College, Dublin (1989). In *Ideology and*

the Historians, edited by Ciaran Brady, 199–210. Dublin: Lilliput Press.

a. Corrected version in *Ideas Matter: Essays in Honour of Conor Cruise O'Brien*, edited by Richard English and Joseph Morrison Skelly, 195–210. Dublin: Poolbeg.

2. "'Fictio,' or the Purposes of Historical Statements." Excerpt from *Historical Consciousness*. In *From Texts to Text*, edited by George H. Jensen, 417–21. New York: HarperCollins.
3. "A New World Is Opening Up." *New Hampshire International Seminar*, Center for International Perspectives, University of New Hampshire, Durham, New Hampshire, 1–22.
4. "Response." In *The Opening of the Second World War: Proceedings of the Second International Conference on International Relations, Held at the American University of Paris, September 26–30, 1989*, edited by David W. Pike, part 1, 56–58. New York: Peter Lang. See also, "Excerpts from the Debate," part 1, 61–62, and "Excerpts from the Debate," part 5, 242–45.
5. "The Greatest Danger Ahead: Soviet Breakup." *Arizona Republic*, January 20: sec. C, 2.
6. "The Ultimate Urban Village." *Mid-Atlantic*, February: 36ff.
7. "The Short Century—It's Over." *New York Times*, February 17: sec. E, 13.
   a. Reprinted in *Readings in Global History*, vol. 2, edited by Anthony Snyder and Sherri West, 322–24. Dubuque, IA: Kendall/Hunt, 1992.
8. "Berlin Letter." *Harper's*, March: 66–70.
9. "Churchill és Magyarország." *Élet és Irodalom*, April 5: 5.
   a. Reprinted as appendix to *A párviadal* (Hungarian edition of *The Duel*). Budapest: Európa Könvykiadó, 1993.
10. "The 'Other Europe' at Century's End." *Wilson Quarterly* (Autumn): 116–22.
11. "The Church in Hungary Today." *America*, October 5: 219–21.
12. "Concept and Symbol of Europe." *New Hungarian Quarterly* (Winter): 3–7.
13. "About the Psychology of the Émigré." *Hungarian Studies*, no. 2: 37–41.
14. "The Transatlantic Duel: Hitler vs. Roosevelt." *American Heritage*, December: 70–77.

1992

1. "America and Russia, Americans and Russians." *American Heritage*, February/March: 64–73.
    a. Reprinted in *New Directions for American History*, vol. 2, edited by Robert James Maddox, 230–35. Guilford, CT: Dushkin Publishing Group, 1993.
2. "The Restaurant Time Forgot." *Town and Country*, May: 68ff.
3. "A párviadal." Excerpts from the Hungarian edition of *The Duel. Nagyvilág*, May: 675–95.
4. "The Patriotic Impulse." Acceptance speech for the Ingersoll Award (1991). *Chronicles*, July: 18–20.
    a. Reprinted as "The Patriotic Identity." In *Immigration and the American Identity: Selections from* Chronicles, *1985–1995*, edited by The Rockford Institute, 197–202. Rockford, IL: Rockford Institute, 1995.
5. "Finland Vindicated." *Foreign Affairs* (Fall): 50–63.
    a. Translated into Hungarian as "A megörzött Finnország." *Európai Szemle*, no. 1 (1993): 101–10.
6. "American History: The Terminological Problem." *American Scholar* (Winter): 17–32.
    a. Pursuant correspondence: (Summer): 634–36.
    b. Translated into Hungarian as "Amerikai történelem, A terminológiai probléma." *Világosság*, no. 6: 409–19.
7. "Christians and the Temptations of Nationalism." Excerpt from *The End of the Twentieth Century. New Oxford Review*, November: 12–17.

1993

1. "Henry Adams and the European Tradition of the Philosophy of History." In *Henry Adams and His World*, edited by David R. Contosta and Robert Muccigrosso, 322–24. Philadelphia: American Philosophical Society.
2. "Western Civilization/European/Christian: What Did They Mean 500 Years Ago? What Do They Mean Today?" *Providence: Studies in Western Civilization* (Summer): 429–37.
3. "History: The Bearer of Culture." In *Studiosorum Speculum: Studies in Honor of Louis J. Léka, O. Cist*, edited by Francis R. Swietek and John R. Sommerfeldt, 263–72. Kalamazoo, MI: Cistercian Publications.

4. "Adenauers Deutschland zwischen Ost und West." In *Nach–Denken: Über Konrad Adenauer und seine Politik*, by Haus der Geschichte der Bundesrepublik Deutschland, 64–74. Bonn: Bouvier, 64–74.
5. "Hitler és Magyarország: A kutatás megválaszolandó kérdései." After: "Jodl vezérörnagy feljegyzései az 1944. március 19 és október 15 események elökészitéséröl." *Századok*, nos. 5 and 6: 750–60.
6. "The End of the Twentieth Century: A Historian's Reflection." *Harper's*, January: 39–58.
7. "History, Wild History." *New York Times*, January 8: sec. A, 25.
    a. Reprinted in *Toronto Globe and Mail*, January 18.
8. "Our Seven Deadly Sins of Misdiagnosis." *Arizona Republic*, January 17: sec. C, 1.
9. "Letter from the Baltics: Cold Comfort." *Chronicles*, February: 39–42.
    a. Corrections in *Chronicles*, June: 4.
10. "Prime Time in Budapest." *Los Angeles Times Magazine*, March 7: 36ff.
11. "Herbert Hoover Meets Adolf Hitler." *American Scholar* (Spring): 235–38.
    a. Pursuant correspondence: (Fall): 634–36.
12. "Atom Smasher Is Super Nonsense." *New York Times*, June 17, sec. A, 25.
13. "Philadelphia: A City of Neighborhoods." *Welcome, America* (Philadelphia Convention Center), June 25–July 5.
14. "How Certain Foreigners Saw New York." *City Journal* (Autumn): 104–9.
15. "Churchill és Magyarország." Excerpt from the Hungarian edition of *The Duel*. *Magyar Nemzet*, September 4.
16. "Horthy Miklós, 1868–1957." *Magyar Hirlap*, September 4.
17. "1918." *American Heritage*, November: 46–51.
18. "Zermatt: Little Town under a Big Mountain." *New York Times*, November 14, Sophisticated Traveler section, 22ff.
19. "Two Worlds." Excerpt from *The End of the Twentieth Century*. *Hungarian Quarterly* (Winter): 76–93.

1994

1. "Barcza György irott hagyatéka." In *Barcza György: Diplomata emlékeim, 1911–1945*, vol. 2. Budapest: Európa-Historia, 239–43.
2. "An Exceptional Mind, an Exceptional Friend." In *The Unbought Grace of Life: Essays in Honor of Russell Kirk*, edited by James E. Person, 51–54. Peru, IL: Sherwood Sugden, 1994.

3. "Kérdések a sajtószabadság és a demokrácia történelméröl." *Magyar Hirlap*, January 4.
4. "Oroszország a határvidék." Hungarian translations of excerpts from *The End of the Twentieth Century*. *Nagyvilág*, no. 4: 338–49.
5. "Tiger, Tigre: The Perils of Translation." *Chronicles*, April: 48.
6. "Benito Mussolini." *New York Times Magazine*, July 24: 14–17.
7. "Revising the Twentieth Century." *American Heritage*, September: 83–89.
   a. Translated into Hungarian as "A huszadik század reviziója." *Világosság*, no. 6, 1995: 63–70.
8. "To Hell with Culture." *Chronicles*, September: 16–19.
   a. Translated into Hungarian as "Pokolba a kulturával." *Európai Szemle*, no. 1, 1995: 11–19.
   b. Reprinted in *Chronicles*, July 2001, 13–15.
9. "Éhes farkas a nyáj között." *Népszabadság*, November 5.
   a. Also published as "Magyarország és a nagyhatalmak 1945–ben." In *Nagy Ferenc miniszterelnök*, edited by István Csicsery-Rónay, 135–38. Budapest: Occidental Press, 1995.

1995

1. "The Meaning of World War II." In *The Americana Annual, 1995: An Encyclopedia of the Events of 1994*, a yearbook of *Encyclopedia Americana*, 567–72. Danbury, CT: Grolier, 567–72.
2. "Off to Off-Season France." *Los Angeles Times*, January 22: sec. L, 1.
3. "Reason and Unreason in Civil Defense." *International Journal of Politics, Culture, and Society* (Spring): 507–10.
4. "Neither the Wilderness nor the Shopping Mall." *New Oxford Review*, April: 6–8.
5. "Letter from Normandy." *American Scholar* (Summer): 359–70.

1996

1. Excerpts from *George F. Kennan and the Origins of Containment, 1944–1946: The Kennan-Lukacs Correspondence*. *Külpolitika*, 106–9.
2. "Our Enemy, the State?" *Wilson Quarterly* (Spring): 108–16.
3. "Phoenixville Needs a Rebuilding of a Small Town Atmosphere—Not a New Mall." *Phoenix* (Phoenixville, PA), May 31: sec. A, 4.
4. "Only in Hungary: The Owl's Castle." *Saveur*, May/June: 26.

5. "Varga Bela életútjáról, halála után egy évvel." *Magyar Nemzet*, November.
6. "A Spa for All Seasons." *New York Times Magazine*, November 10: Sophisticated Traveler section, 54ff.
7. "Goodbye (and Hello) to All That." *Newsday*, December 29: sec. A, 39.

1997

1. "Fear and Hatred." *American Scholar* (Summer): 437–41.
    a. Translated into Hungarian as "Félelem és gyülölet." *Korunk* (Cluj) no. 10: 111–16.
2. "Churchill the Visionary." The Fourteenth Crosby Kemper Lecture, Winston Churchill Memorial, Westminster College, Fulton, Missouri, April 13.
3. "A vallás és a történettudomány." *Vigilia* (Budapest), May: 384–90. Also: Interview with John Lukacs, 330–45.
4. "The Idea that Remade Europe." *Washington Post*, May 25, sec. C, 3.
5. "Moral und die Kunst des Möglichen: Betrachtungen eines amerikanischen Historikers zur Schweiz." *Neue Zürcher Zeitung*, July 31.
    a. Translated into English as "Morality and the Art of the Possible." *Swiss Review of World Affairs* (October): 28–30.
6. Excerpts from *A Thread of Years*, with a special introduction. *Hungarian Quarterly* (Autumn): 13–29.
7. "To Hell with College." *Chronicles*, September: 14–17.
8. "The Folly of Higher Education." *Arizona Republic*, September 14, sec. H, 1–3.

1998

1. "Conservatives Also Oppose Development that Destroys Farms and Neighborhoods." *Phoenix* (Phoenixville, PA), January 23: sec. A, 4.
2. "The Texture of Time." Excerpt from *A Thread of Years*. *American Heritage*, February/March, 68–72.
3. "A rövid évszázad után." *Magyar Hirlap*, March 28.
4. "The Meaning of '98." *American Heritage*, May/June: 72–80.
5. Excerpts from *A történelmi Hitler*. *Népszabadság*, June 6.
6. "Vallomások Budapeströl." *Uj Magyar Építömüvészet*, no. 5: 13–14.
7. "Dwight Macdonald." *Chronicles*, November: 14–16.

8. "Teaching American History." *American Scholar* (Winter): 100–101.

1999

1. "Der Zweite Weltkrieg: In Schutt und Asche." In *Spiegel des 20. Jahrhunderts*, edited by Dieter Wild, 175–86. Hamburg: Spiegel-Buchverlag.
    a. "Der Zweite Weltkrieg: In Schutt und Asche." *Der Spiegel*, January 25: 116–25.
2. "Historical Revisionism about the Origins of the Wars of the Twentieth Century." In *War, Resistance, and Intelligence: Essays in Honor of M. R. D. Foot*, edited by K. G. Robertson, 71–82. Barnsley: Leo Cooper/Pen and Sword Books.
3. "The Reality of Written Words." *Chronicles*, January: 43–45.
4. "A roved évszázad után." *Forrás*, January: 6–9.
5. "*Évek* . . ." Excerpts from Hungarian translation of *A Thread of Years*. *Nagyvilág*, March/April: 216, 245.
6. "The Anderson Cemetery on Valley Park Road." *Schuylkill Township News* (Chester County, PA), Spring: 3.
7. "The Poverty of Anti-Communism." With responses from Robert Conquest, William F. Buckley Jr., and Nathan Glazer. *National Interest* (Spring): 75–86.
    a. Author's responses to Conquest, Buckley, and Glazer: (Summer): 149.
8. "Magyarország a hazám, Amerika az otthonom." *Magyar Nemzet*, June 5.
9. "Erik von Kuehnelt-Leddihn: A Memoir." *Intercollegiate Review* (Fall): 34–36.
10. "Austria." *New York Times Magazine*, November 21, Sophisticated Traveler section, 14–16.

2000

1. "Az Európa–fogalom kialakulàsa és fejlödése: Magyarorszàg helye Európàban." In *A hid tulsó oldalan. Tanulmányok Kelet–Közép Európáról*, edited by Bàn D. András, 9–43. Budapest: Osiris.
2. "1849: az európai forradalmak kora lezárult." *Nagyvilág* (Budapest), nos. 1 and 2: 90–96.
    a. Reprinted in *Magyar Nemzet* (Budapest), February 26: 7.

3. "The Trolley Park at Valley Forge." *Schuylkill Township News* (Chester County, PA), Spring: 3.
4. "The Price of Defending Hitler: A Historian Explains Why a Leading Voice of 'Holocaust Denial' Lost His Libel Case." *Newsweek*, April 24: 4.
5. "Elian Editorial Was Right on the Mark." *Phoenix* (Phoenixville, PA), May 1, sec. A, 4.
6. "Magyarország a huszadik században." *Magyar Nemzet* (Budapest), July 8.
7. "The Tragedy of Two Hungarian Prime Ministers." *Hungarian Quarterly* (Budapest), (Autumn): 77–83.
8. "The Pickering Reservoir." *Schuylkill Township News* (Chester County, PA), Autumn: 3.

2001

1. "*The Great Gatsby*? Yes, a Historical Novel." In *Novel History: Historians and Novelists Confront America's Past (and Each Other)*, edited by Mark C. Carnes, 235–58. New York: Simon and Schuster.
2. "Ëgy borivó vallomásai." In *Alibi hat h napra*, edited by Alexander Bródy, 9–13. Budapest: Alibi Kiado, 2001.
3. "The Election of Theodore Roosevelt, 1912." In *What If? Eminent Historians Imagine What Might Have Been*, edited by Robert Cowley, 181–94. New York: Putnam.
    a. Paperbound edition: 2002.
4. "Magyar Katolikovok és a zsidókérdés." *Vigilia*, no. 9.
5. "Brandy Old and Great: Armagnac Is Making a Comeback . . ." *Saveur*, January/February: 27–29. (Article badly mangled by editors.)
6. "The Population History of Schuylkill Township." *Schuylkill Township News* (Chester County, PA), Spring: 3.
7. "America's Venice." *American Heritage*, April: 42–49.
8. "Accumulating New Wealth." Commencement address delivered at Stonehill College. *Stonehill Alumni Magazine*, May 22: 33.
9. "Fény Keletröl. Húsvet Varsóban." Excerpts from the Hungarian translation of *Destinations Past*. *Nagyvilág*, no. 6: 879–90.
10. "Churchill the Visionary." Address at the Churchill Society for the Advancement of Parliamentary Democracy, Toronto, Canada, November 28, 2000. Published as pamphlet.

2002

1. "The Fifties: Another View: Revising the Eisenhower Era." *Harper's*, January: 64–70.
2. "It's the End of the Modern Age." Excerpt from chapter one of *At the End of an Age*. *Chronicle of Higher Education*, April 26, sec. B, 7–11.
3. "Mechanic." *American Scholar* (Winter): 107–10.
4. "The Old Pickering Schoolhouse." *Schuylkill Township News* (Chester County, PA), Spring: 3.
5. "Párt, nemzet, nép." *Népszabadság* (Budapest), April 13: 25.
6. "The Copenhagen Question: Why Did the Nazis Drop the A-Bomb?" *Daily Telegraph* (London), June 12: 18.
7. "Popular and Professional History." *Historically Speaking*, April: 2–5.
8. "The Universality of National Socialism." *Totalitarian Movements and Political Religions* (London) (Summer): 107–21.
    a. Translated into Hungarian as "A nemzetiszocializmus egyetemes jellege." *Klió*, no. 1, 2003: 8–21.
9. "Education, Schooling, Learning: To Hell with Communications." *Chronicles*, September: 17–18.
10. "Hitler's War Years." In *One of Freedom's Finest Hours: Statesmanship and Soldiership in World War II*, edited by Joseph H. Alexander and Larry P. Arnn, 119–28. Hillsdale, MI: Hillsdale College Press.
11. "The Churchill-Roosevelt Forgeries." *American Heritage*, November/December: 65–67.
12. "Menton: Quiet Days and Silent Nights." *New York Times*, November 17, Sophisticated Traveler section, 40–44, 65, 72.
13. Summary of lecture, "The Condition of History." In *Aktuellt om Historia 2002: De svenska historiedagarna í Göteborg 5–7 Oktober 2001*, edited by Göran Olsson, 13–16.
14. "The Obsolescence of the American Intellectual." *Chronicle of Higher Education* October 4: sec. B, 7–10.

2003

1. "Egy någy államferfi érdeklödése Magyarorszá iránt." *Kritika*, February: 29–31.
2. "What *Is* History?" *Historically Speaking*, February: 9–12.

a. Translated into Hungarian as "Mi a történelem." *Klió*, no. 3, 3–10.

3. "Historians and the Cold War." In *The Cold War: Opening Shots 1945–1950*. Lexington, VA: Virginia Military Institute, 35–43.
4. "A Senseless Salute." *New York Times*, April 14, sec. A, 19.
   a. Reprinted in *International Herald Tribune*, April 16: 9.
   b. Reprinted in *Neue Zürcher Zeitung*, May 4: 22.
   c. Reprinted in *Válasz* (Budapest), April 25.
   d. Reprinted in *Hintergrund*, May 4: 22.
5. "Fürdökádakról." *Alibi*, no. 4: 95–98.
6. "Stella. De Mégis . . ." *Alibi*, no. 5: 10–13.
7. "No Pearl Harbor? FDR Delays the War." In *What Ifs? of American History: Eminent Historians Imagine What Might Have Been*, edited by Robert Cowley, 179–88. New York: G. P. Putnam.
8. "A Final Chapter on Churchill." *Chronicle Review*, October 24, sec. B, 7–10.

Part III: Reviews

1948

1. Review of *Christianity and America*, by John J. Meng and Emro Joseph Gergely. *Liturgical Arts*, August: 126.
2. Review of *Kossuth Lajos a reformkorban*, by Domokos Kosáry. *Journal of Modern History* (December): 347–48.

1949

1. Review of *The Cardinal's Story*, by Stephen K. Swift. Under the pseudonym "Luke Ungern." *Thought*, March: 571–72.
2. Review of *Mezögazdaság és agrártársadalom Magyarországon*, by Gyula Mérei. *Journal of Central European Affairs* (January): 425–26.
3. Review of *Forradalom után*, by Gyula Szekfü. *American Slavic and East European Review* (February): 73–75.
4. Review of *Chronology of the Second World War*, by the Royal Institute of International Affairs. *Journal of Modern History* (March): 69.

5. Review of *Mindszenty—The True Story of the Heroic Cardinal of Hungary*, by Nicholas Boer. *Philadelphia Catholic Standard and Times*, July 15: 8.
6. Review of *Immigrant Life in New York City, 1825–1863*, by Robert Ernst. *Pennsylvania Magazine of History and Biography*, October: 525–26.

1950

1. Review of *Vorspiel zum Krieg im Osten*, by Grigore Gafencu. *Journal of Central European Affairs*: 219–21.
2. Review of four books by and about Cardinal Mindszenty. Under the pseudonym "Luke Ungern." *Thought*: 681–83.

1951

1. Review of *La guerre germano-soviétique 1941–1945*, by A. Guillaume. *American Slavic and East European Review* (December): 308–10.

1953

1. Review of *A House on Bryanston Square*, by Algernon Cecil. *Commonweal*, February 27: 530.
2. Review of *The Genius of American Politics*, by Daniel J. Boorstin. *Commonweal*, July 24: 397–98.
3. Review of *Soviet Imperialism: Its Origin and Tactics*, edited by Waldemar Gurian. *Commonweal*, July 31: 426.
4. Review of *Beyond Containment*, by William Henry Chamberlain. *Commonweal*, October 16: 43.

1954

1. Review of *Une mancata intesa italo-sovietica nel 1940 e 1941*, by Mario Toscano. *American Historical Review* (January): 413.
2. Review of *Challenge in Eastern Europe*, edited by C. E. Black. *Catholic Historical Review* (January): 58–59.
3. Review of *Triumph and Tragedy: The Second World War*, vol. 6, by Winston Churchill. *Commonweal*, January 1: 335–36.

4. Review of *Queen Victoria and Her Prime Ministers*, by Algernon Cecil. *Commonweal*, January 8: 358–59.
5. Review of *World Power in the Balance*, by Tibor Mende. *Commonweal*, March 5: 562–63.
6. Review of *Melbourne*, by Lord David Cecil. *Commonweal*, December 10: 293–94.

1955

1. Review of *A Program for Conservatives*, by Russell Kirk. *Social Order*, May: 231–32.

1956

1. Review of *Czartoryski and European Unity, 1770–1861*, by M. Kukiel. *Catholic Historical Review* (April): 74–75.

1957

1. Review of *Alexis de Tocqueville: The Critical Years, 1848–1851*, by Edward Gargan. *The Journal of Modern History* (June): 138–39.
2. Review of *Ouevres complètes*, by Alexis de Tocqueville, edited by J. P. Mayer, André Jardin, and Gustave Rudler. Paris: Gallimard: 1952–. (Review covers Tomb 1, *De la démocratie en Amérique*; Tomb 2, *L'Ancien régime et la révolution*, including *Fragments et notes inedited sur la revolution*; and Tomb 6, *Correspondence anglaise*.) *Journal of Modern History* (September): 280–84.

1958

1. Review of *On the Philosophy of History*, by Jacques Maritain. *National Review*, January 4: 20–21.
2. Review of *Philadelphia Gentlemen: The Making of a National Upper Class*, by E. Digby Baltzell. *National Review*, April 19: 380–81.
3. Review of *Winston Churchill and the Second Front, 1940–43*, by Trumbull Higgins. *New Leader*, May 12: 21–22.
4. Review of *Meinungsforschung und repräsentative Demokratie*, by Wilhelm Hennis. *Journal of Modern History* (September): 271.

1959

1. Review of *Oucvres complètes*, by Alexis de Tocqueville, edited by J. P. Mayer, André Jardin, Maurice Degros, et al. Paris: Gallimard: 1952–. (Review covers Tomb 5, v01.1, *Voyages en Sicile et aux États-Unis*; and vol. 2, *Voyages en Angleterre, Irlande, Suisse, et Algerie.*) Also reviewed is *Alexis de Tocqueville's Amerikabild*, by Bernhard Fabian. Heidelberg: C. Winter, 1957. *Journal of Modern History* (March): 57–60.

1960

1. Review of *Comte de Gobineau–Mère Benedicte de Gobineau: Correspondence, 1872–1883*, edited by A. B. Duff and R. Rancoeur. *Catholic Historical Review* (January): 473–75.
2. Review of *Alexis de Tocqueville in the Chamber of Deputies: His Views on Foreign and Colonial Policy*, by Sister Mary Lawlor. *Review of Politics* (April): 284–86.
3. Review of *Ouevres complètes*, by Alexis de Tocqueville, edited by J. P. Mayer, André Jardin, Maurice Degros, et al. Paris: Gallimard, 1952–. (Review covers Tomb 9, *Correspondence de Alexis de Tocqueville et d'Arthur de Gobineau.*) *Journal of Modern History* (September): 296–97.

1962

1. Review of *Bernanos—His Political Thought and Prophecy*, by Thomas Molnar. *Dokumente* (Cologne), April: 151–52.

1963

1. Review of *The French Army: A Military-Political History*, by Paul Marie de la Gorce, and *Dare Call It Treason*, by Richard M. Watt. *New York Review of Books*, June 1: 36–38.
2. Review of *Tocqueville and the Old Regime*, by Richard Herr. *Catholic Historical Review* (January): 546–47.
3. Review of *German Catholics and Hitler's Wars*, by Gordon Zahn. *Review of Politics* (April): 241–43.

1964

1. Review of *The End of Alliance*, by Ronald Steel, and *The Politics of the Atlantic Alliance*, by Alvin J. Cottrell and James E. Dougherty. *Worldview*, July/August: 13–15.
2. Review of *The Fall of the House of Hapsburg*, by Edward Crankshaw, and *The Anschluss*, by Gordon Brook-Shepherd. *Review of Politics* (October): 547–51.

1965

1. Review of *Pétain et de Gaulle*, by J. R. Tournoux. *Die Zeit* (Hamburg), March 12: 43.
2. Review of *The Historian and History*, by Page Smith. *Catholic Historical Review* (April): 65–67.
3. Review of *Power at the Pentagon*, by Jack Raymond. *Die Zeit* (Hamburg), May 7: 30.

1966

1. Review of *Under Their Vine and Fig Tree: Travels through America in 1797–1799, 1805, with Some Further Account of Life in New Jersey*, by Julian Ursyn Niemcewicz, edited and translated by M. J. E. Budka. *Pennsylvania Magazine of History and Biography*, January: 90–91.
2. Review of *Letters of Oswald Spengler, 1913–1936. New York Times Book Review*, March 6: 6.

1967

1. Review of *Mussolini il revoluzionario*, 1883–1920, by Renzo De Felice. *American Historical Review* (April): 1027–28.
2. Review of *The War Years, 1939–1945*, vol. 2, *Diaries and Letters*, by Harold Nicolson. *Saturday Review*, June 17: 27–28.
3. Review of *An Introduction to Contemporary History*, by Geoffrey Barraclough. *Catholic Historical Review* (October): 432–33.
4. Review of *In Search of the Modern World*, by Robert Sinai. New York Times Book Review, October 22: 22–24.
5. Review of *Memoirs, 1925–1950*, by George F. Kennan. *New Republic*, October 28: 28–31.

6. Review of *After Victory: Churchill, Roosevelt, Stalin, and the Making of Peace*, by William L. Neumann. *Progressive*, December: 42–44.

1968

1. Review of *Säkularisierung: Geschichte eines ideenpolitischen Begriffs*, by Hermann Lübbe. *Catholic Historical Review* (January): 731–32.
2. Review of *Three Faces of Fascism: Action Française, Italian Fascism, National Socialism*, by Ernst Nolte. *Catholic Historical Review* (October): 521.
3. Review of *Der Marschall. Pétain zwischen Kollaboration und Resistance*, by Pierre Bourget. *Die Zeit* (Hamburg), October 18.
4. Review of *History of the Cold War: From the October Revolution to the Korean War, 1917–1950*, by André Fontaine. *Interplay: The Magazine of International Affairs*, November: 54–55.

1969

1. Review of *The Fate of the Revolution: Interpretations of Soviet History: The Impact of the Russian Revolution, 1917–1967*, by Walter Laqueur. Also reviewed is *Revolutionary Russia: A Symposium*, edited by Richard Pipes. *Problems of Communism* (January/February): 35–37.
2. Review of *Why France Fell*, by Guy Chapman, and *To Lose a Battle*, by Alistair Horne. *Commonweal*, August 22: 520–21.

1971

1. Review of *The Onset of the Cold War, 1945–1950*, by Herbert Feis. *National Review*, February 9: 152–53.
2. Review of *The Danube Swabians*, by G. C. Paikert. *Catholic Historical Review* (April): 144–46.
3. Review of *Ten Years After: The Hungarian Revolution in the Perspective of History*, edited by Tamás Aczél. *Catholic Historical Review* (July): 357.

1972

1. Review of *The Nature of Civilizations*, by Matthew Melko, and *Timeless Problems in History*, by Bernard Norling. *American Historical Review* (October): 1083.

2. Review of *The Coming of Age*, by Simone de Beauvoir. *Triumph*, December: 37.

1973

1. Review of *Timeless Problems in History*, by Bernard Norling. *Catholic Historical Review* (July): 304–5.
2. Review of *Aid to Russia, 1941–1946: Strategy, Diplomacy, and the Origins of the Cold War*, by George C. Herring. *History: Reviews of New Books*, August: 197.
3. Review of *Dilemmas of Democracy: Tocqueville and Modernization*, by Seymour Drescher. *Catholic Historical Review* (October): 428–29.

1974

1. Review of *Fél évszázad*, by Paul Auer. *East Central Europe* 1: 111.
2. Review of *Has the Catholic Church Gone Mad*? by John Eppstein. *Christian Scholars Review* 4, no. 2: 156–57.
3. "The Diplomacy of the Holy See during World War II." Review-article of the series *Actes et documents du Saint Siège relatifs à la Seconde Guerre Mondiale*, edited by Pierre Blet, Robert A. Graham, Angelo Martini, and Burkhart Schneider. Vatican City: Libreria editrice vaticana, 1965–67. (Review covers vol. 6, *Le Saint Siège et les victimes de la guerre, Mars 1939–Décembre 1940*, and vol. 7, *Le Saint Siège et la guerre mondiale, Novembre 1942–Décembre 1943*. *Catholic Historical Review* (July): 271–78. (See also related entries in Reviews: 1976, 1979, 1983.)
4. Review of *Aneurin Bevan: A Biography*, vol. 2, 1945–60, by Michael Foot. *History: Reviews of New Books*, August: 231.
5. Review of *Race to Pearl Harbor: The Failure of the Second London Conference and the Onset of World War II*, by Stephen E. Pelz. *History: Reviews of New Books*, November/December: 14.

1975

1. Review of *Another Part of the Wood: A Self-Portrait*, by Kenneth Clark. *Philadelphia Sunday Bulletin*, May 18, sec. 4.
2. Review-essay of *Clio and the Doctors*, by Jacques Barzun. *Salmagundi* (Summer): 93–106.

1976

1. Review of *In Search of Europe*, by Guido Piovene. *New York Times Book Review*, February 22: 2ff.
2. Review of *The Complete Works of Saki. New York Times Book Review*, March 28: 6ff.
3. Review of *Uncle of Europe: The Social and Diplomatic Life of Edward VII*, by Gordon Brook-Shepherd. *National Review*, May 28: 572–73.
4. Review-article of *Actes et documents du Saint Siège relatifs à la Seconde Guerre Mondiale*, edited by Pierre Blet, Robert A. Graham, Angelo Martini, and Burkhart Schneider. Vatican City: Libreria editrice vaticana, 1965–67. (Review covers vol. 8, *Le Saint Siège et les victimes de la guerre. Janvier 1941-Décembre 1942.*) *Catholic Historical Review* (October): 667–68.
5. Review of *The Damnable Question: One Hundred and Twenty Years of Anglo-Irish Conflict*, by George Dangerfield. *National Review*, November 12: 1244–45.

1977

1. Review-essay of *Histoire et historiens: Une mutation idéologique des historiens français, 1865–1885*, by Charles-Oliver Carbonell. *Salmagundi* (Spring): 155–60.
2. Review of *Three French Writers and the Great War: Studies in the Rise of Communism and Fascism*, by Frank Field. *New Oxford Review*, May: 21–22.
3. Review of *Hitler's War*, by David Irving. *National Review*, August 19: 946–50.

1978

1. Review of *Interpretations of Fascism*, by Renzo de Felice. *New Oxford Review*, May: 21.
2. Review of *Final Entries 1945: The Diaries of Joseph Goebbels*, edited by Hugh Trevor-Roper. *National Review*, December 8: 50–51.

1979

1. Review-article of *Actes et documents du Saint Siège relatifs à la Seconde Guerre Mondiale*, edited by Pierre Blet, Robert A. Graham,

Angelo Martini, and Burkhart Schneider. Vatican City: Libreria editrice vaticana, 1965–67. (Review covers vol. 9, *Le Saint Siège et les victimes de la guerre, Janvier 1941–Décembre 1943.*) *Catholic Historical Review* (January): 92–94.

2. Review of *Adventures of a Bystander*, by Peter F. Drucker. *American Spectator*, September: 34.
3. Review of *The Old Patagonian Express: By Train through the Americas*, by Paul Theroux. *National Review*, October 26: 1372–74.
4. Review of *White House Years*, by Henry Kissinger. *Philadelphia Inquirer*, November 18, sec. 1, 14.

1980

1. Review of *The Advent of War, 1939–1940*, by Roy Douglas. *American Historical Review* (February): 117.
2. Review of *Arabia*, by Jonathan Raban. *National Review*, June 27: 792–93.
3. Review of *Empire as a Way of Life*, by William Appleman Williams. *New Republic*, October 11: 31–33.
4. Review of *Fire in the Minds of Men: Origins of the Revolutionary Faith*, by James H. Billington. *National Review*, November 28: 1465.

1981

1. Review of *The Letters of Evelyn Waugh*, edited by Mark Amory. *National Review*, January 23: 41–44.
2. Review of *The War between the Generals: Inside the Allied High Command*, by David Irving. *New York Times Sunday Book Review*, March 8: 12–13, 27.
3. Review of *Off the Record: The Private Papers of Harry S. Truman*, by Robert H. Ferrell. *Philadelphia Inquirer Sunday Book Review.*
4. Review of *Monty: The Making of a General*, by Nigel Hamilton. *Business Week*, September 28: 15–17.
5. Review of *The Politics of Genocide: The Holocaust in Hungary*, vols. 1 and 2, by Randolph B. Braham. *History: Reviews of New Books*, October: 22–23.
6. "History with a Difference." Review of *God's Fifth Column: The Biography of an Age, 1880–1940*, by William Gerhardie. *New York Times Sunday Book Review*, November 29: 9.

1982

1. "Galbraith Unhooked." *American Spectator*, February: 29–44. (Correspondence about Sidney Hook's October 1981 article on *A Life in Our Times: Memoirs*, by John Kenneth Galbraith, followed by Hook's reply to Lukacs.)

1983

1. Review-article of *Actes et documents du Saint Siège relatifs à la Seconde Guerre Mondiale*, edited by Pierre Blet, Robert A. Graham, Angelo Martini, and Burkhart Schneider. Vatican City: Libreria editrice vaticana, 1965–67. (Review covers vol. 10, *Le Saint Siège et les victimes de la guerre: Janvier 1944–Juillet 1945.*) *Catholic Historical Review* (January): 81–83.
2. Review of *Growing Up*, by Russell Baker. *National Review*, March 18: 331–32.
3. Review of *In War's Dark Shadow—The Russians before the Great War*, by W. Bruce Lincoln. *Detroit News*, May 18: sec. A, 13.
4. Review-article of *Actes et documents du Saint Siège relatifs à la Seconde Guerre Mondiale*, edited by Pierre Blet, Robert A. Graham, Angelo Martini, and Burkhart Schneider. Vatican City: Libreria editrice vaticana, 1965–67. (Review covers vol. 11, *Le Saint Siège et les victimes de la guerre: Janvier 1944–Mai 1945.*) *Catholic Historical Review* (July): 414–19.
5. Review of *Like It Was: The Diaries of Malcolm Muggeridge*, by Malcolm Muggeridge. *New Republic*, July 18–25: 37–39.

1984

1. Review of *The Vatican and Hungary, 1846–1878: Reports and Correspondence on Hungary of the Apostolic Nuncios in Vienna*, by Lajos Lukács. *Catholic Historical Review* (July): 496–97.
2. Review of *At Dawn We Slept: The Untold Story of Pearl Harbor*, by Gordon W. Prange; *Infamy: Pearl Harbor and Its Aftermath*, by John Toland; *The Pacific War*, by John Costello; and *The American Magic: Codes, Ciphers, and the Defeat of Japan*, by Ronald Lewin. *National Review*, July 9: 840–42.
3. Review of *Vita: A Biography of Vita Sackville-West*, by Victoria Glendenning. *National Review*, September 21: 50–52.

4. Review of *The Past Recaptured: Great Historians and the History of History*, by M. A. Fitzsimons. *Review of Politics* (October): 607–9.
5. Review of *One More Day's Journey*, by Allen B. Ballard. *Philadelphia*, December: 119–20.

1985

1. Review of *Revisionism and Empire: Socialist Imperialism in Germany, 1897–1915*, by Roger Fletcher. *History: Reviews of New Books*, January: 67.
2. Review of *How Democracies Perish*, by Jean-François Revel. *Philadelphia Inquirer*, January 27: sec. P, 1, 6.
3. Review of *Before the Trumpet: Young Franklin Roosevelt 1882–1905*, by Geoffrey C. Ward. *Philadelphia Inquirer*, May 26: sec. P, 1.
4. Review of *Between Russia and the West: Hungary and the Illusions of Peacemaking, 1945–1947*, by Stephen D. Kertesz. *National Review*, May 31: 52–53.
5. Review of *Harold Nicolson*, by James Lees-Milne. *New Yorker*, September 2: 82–86.
6. Review of *Churchill and Roosevelt: The Complete Correspondence*, edited by Warren F. Kimball. *New Yorker*, September 16: 114–22.
7. Review of *The Liberal Mind in a Conservative Age: American Intellectuals in the 1940s and 1950s*, by Richard H. Pells. *Chronicles of Culture*, October: 8–10.

1986

1. Review of *Vichy France and the Resistance: Culture and Ideology*, edited by H. R. Kedward and Roger Austin. *History: Reviews of New Books*, January/February: 79–80.
2. Review of *Son of the Morning Star*, by Evan S. Connell. *Chronicles*, May: 31–40.
3. Review of *Sacco and Vanzetti: The Case Resolved*, by Francis Russell. *National Review*, May 23: 42.
4. Review of *Monte Cassino*, edited by David Hapgood and David Richardson. *Catholic Historical Review* (July): 471.
5. Review of *Alexis de Tocqueville: Selected Letters on Politics and Society*, edited by Roger Boesche. *Chronicles*, September: 29–30.
6. Review of *Home: A Short History of an Idea*, by Witold Rybczynski. *New Yorker*, September 1: 96–99.

7. Review of *Philadelphia on the River*, by Philip Chadwick Foster Smith. *Pennsylvania Magazine of History and Biography*, October: 585.
8. Review of *Forgotten Allies: The Military Contribution of the Colonies, Exiled Governments, and Lesser Powers to the Allied Victory in World War II*, by J. Lee Ready. *American Historical Review* (October): 885.

1987

1. Review of *Passage through Armageddon: The Russians in War and Revolution, 1914–1918*, by W. Bruce Lincoln. *World and I*, January: 434–48.
2. Review of *Pio XII*, edited by Andrea Riccardi. *Catholic Historical Review* (January): 120–21.
3. Review of *The Cycles of American History*, by Arthur M. Schlesinger Jr. *Philadelphia Inquirer*, January 11: sec. P, 7.
4. Review of *István Tisza: The Liberal Vision and Conservative Statecraft of a Magyar Nationalist*, by Gábor Vermes. *Catholic Historical Review* (October): 674–75.

1988

1. Review of *The Tenants of Time*, by Thomas Flanagan. *World and I*, June: 441–44.
2. Review of *Die Tagebücher von Joseph Goebbels: Sämtliche Fragmente*, vols. 1–4, 1924–41, edited by Elke Fröhlich. *New York Review of Books*, July 21: 14–17.
3. Review of *Catholics, the State, and the European Radical Right, 1919–1945*, by Richard J. Wolff and Jorg K. Hoensch. *Catholic Historical Review* (October): 645–46.
4. Review of *Tocqueville: A Biography*, by André Jardin. *New Yorker*, November 14: 136–40.
5. Review of *A Certain Climate*, by Paul Horgan. *National Review*, November 25: 47–48.

1989

1. Review of *La Romania nella diplomazia Vaticana*, by Ion Dimitriu-Snagov. *Catholic Historical Review* (April): 343.
2. Review of *Citizens*, by Simon Schama. *National Review*, July 1: 48–50.

3. Review of *The Danube*, by Claudio Magris. *Boston Sunday Globe*, September 24: sec. B, 106–7.

1990

1. Review of *Domenico Tardini, 1888–1961: L'azione della Santa Sede nella crisi fra le due guerre*, by Carlo Felice Casula. *Catholic Historical Review* (April): 396–97.
2. Review of *Threshold of War: Franklin D. Roosevelt and American Entry into World War II*, by Waldo Heinrichs; *Wind over Sand: The Diplomacy of Franklin D. Roosevelt*, by Frederick W. Marks III; *Roosevelt and Stalin: The Failed Courtship*, by Robert Nisbet; and *From War to Cold War: The Education of Harry S. Truman*, by Robert James Maddox. *Virginia Quarterly Review* (Summer): 547–64.

1991

1. Review of *The Churchill-Eisenhower Correspondence, 1953–1955*, edited by Peter G. Boyle. *New York Times Book Review*, February 10: 3–5.
2. Review of *Reworking the Past: Hitler, the Holocaust, and the Historians' Debate*, edited by Peter Baldwin. *History: Reviews of New Books*, Summer: 174.
3. Review of *Stalin: Triumph and Tragedy*, by Dmitri Volkogonov, and *Stalin, Breaker of Nations*, by Robert Conquest. *Boston Globe*, November 10, sec. A, 16.

1992

1. Review of *Bethlen István. Politikai életrajz*, by Ignác Romsics. *New Hungarian Quarterly* (Autumn): 137–39. Hungarian version in *Századok* (1992): 495–96.
2. Review of *Hitler and Stalin: Parallel Lives*, by Alan Bullock. *Philadelphia Inquirer*, March 29.
3. Review of *Church History in the Age of Uncertainty: Historiographical Patterns in the United States, 1906–1990*, by Henry Warner Bowden. *Catholic Historical Review*, (October): 689–90.
4. Review of *The End of History and the Last Man*, by Francis Fukuyama, and *The Democracy Trap: Pitfalls of the Post–Cold War World*, by Graham E. Fuller. *Chronicles*, December: 39–40.

1993

1. Review of *Geschichte der Kirche Osteuropas im 20. Jahrhundert*, by Gabriel Andriányi. *Catholic Historical Review* (January): 143–44.
2. Review of *A Historian and His World: A Life of Christopher Dawson*, by Christina Scott. *Intercollegiate Review* (Spring): 50–52.
3. Review of *Out of Control: Global Turmoil on the Eve of the 21st Century*, by Zbigniew Brzezinski. *Washington Post Book World*, May 16: 9.
4. Review of *Összetört cimerek. A Magyar arisz-tokrácia és az 1945 utáni megpróbáltatások*, by János Gudenus-László Szentirmay. *Hungarian Quarterly* (Summer): 131–34.
5. Review of *Heisenberg's War: The Secret History of the German Bomb*, by Thomas Powers. *Philadelphia Inquirer*, 13 June: sec. H, 2.
6. Review of *Churchill: The End of Glory: A Political Biography*, by John Charmley. *Washington Post Book World*, August 22: 8.

1994

1. Review of *Fra Istanbul, Atene e la Guerra. La missione di A. G. Roncalli, 1935–1944*, by Alberto Melloni. *Catholic Historical Review* (April): 392–93.
2. Review of *The Wrath of Nations: Civilization and the Furies of Nationalism*, by William Pfaff. *Freedom Review*, February: 78–79.

1995

1. Review of *The First World War: A Complete History*, by Martin Gilbert, and *The Origins of War*, by Donald Kagan. *Los Angeles Times Book Review*, January 22: 1.

1996

1. Review of *Anecdotage: A Summation*, by Gregor von Rezzori. *Washington Post Book World*, April 7: 11–12.
2. Review of *Stalin's Letters to Molotov, 1925–1936*, edited by Lars T. Lih, Oleg V. Naumov, and Oleg V. Khlevniuk. *Chronicles*, March: 36–37.
3. Review of *Die amerikanische Besetzung Deutschlands*, by Klaus-Dietmar Henke. *Review of Politics* (Fall): 840–45.

1997

1. Review of *The Unconscious Civilization*, by John Ralston Saul. *Washington Post Book World*, February 2: 8. Pursuant correspondence: March 2: 15.
2. Review of *The Transformation of European Politics, 1763–1848*, by Paul W. Schroeder. *Continuity* (Spring): 121–24.
3. Review of *André Malraux: A Biography*, by Curtis Cate. *Chronicles*, October: 42–44.

1998

1. Review of *Napoleon: A Biography*, by Frank McLynn. *Guardian* (London), February 19: 12.
2. Review of *The Historical Present: Uses and Abuses of the Past*, by Edwin M. Yoder Jr. *Los Angeles Times Book Review*, April 26: 12.
3. Review of *Faust's Metropolis: A History of Berlin*, by Alexandra Ritchie, and *Berlin and Its Culture: A Historical Portrait*, by Ronald Taylor. *Los Angeles Times Book Review*, May 10: 4.
4. Review of *The Dying President: Franklin D. Roosevelt, 1944–1945*, by Robert H. Ferrell. *Los Angeles Times Book Review*, July 26: 9.
5. Review of *Hitler, 1889–1936: Hubris*, by Ian Kershaw. *Spectator* (London), September 19: 39–40.
6. Review of *American Catholic*, by Charles R. Morris. *Pennsylvania History* (Winter): 97–98.

1999

1. Review of *Säkularisierung, Dechristianisierung, Rechristianisierung im neuzeitlichen Europa: Bilanz und Perspektiven der Forschung*, edited by Hartmut Lehmann. *Catholic Historical Review* (January): 81–82.
2. Review of *Secrecy: The American Experience*, by Daniel Patrick Moynihan. *Los Angeles Times Book Review*, January 3: 7.
3. Review of *The Pity of War*, by Niall Ferguson. *Wall Street Journal*, April 14: sec. A, 24.
4. Review of *Anglomania*, by Ian Buruma. *Los Angeles Times Book Review*, June 6: 2.
5. Review of *Hitler's Vienna: A Dictator's Apprenticeship*, by Brigitte Hamann. *Spectator* (London) July 3: 31–32.

6. Review of *The Passing of an Illusion: The Idea of Communism in the Twentieth Century*, by François Furet. *Boston Sunday Globe*, July 4: F3.
7. Review of *Grand Delusion: Stalin and the German Invasion of Russia*, by Gabriel Gorodetsky. *New Republic*, November 15: 47–50.
    a. Translated into Hungarian in *Klió*, no. 3.
8. Review of *Hitler's Pope*, by John Cornwell. *National Review*, November 22: 59–61.

2000

1. Review of *A Republic, Not an Empire: Reclaiming America's Destiny*, by Patrick J. Buchanan. *Chronicles*, January: 29.
2. Review of *Arthur Koestler: The Homeless Mind*, by David Cesarani. *Los Angeles Times Book Review*, January 9: 9.
    a. Translated into Hungarian as *A nyugtalan ember. Magyar Nemzet* (Budapest), March 14.
3. Review of *Holy Madness: Romantics, Patriots, and Revolutionaries, 1776–1871*, by Adam Zamoyski. *Times* (London), February 3: 46.
4. Review of *Copenhagen*, by Michael Frayn. *Los Angeles Times Book Review*, May 12: 6.
    a. Translated into Hungarian as *Heisenberg és Bohr. Világosság* (Budapest), November/December.
5. Review of *Churchill and Appeasement*, by R. A. C. Parker. *Spectator* (London), July 22: 32–33.
6. Review of *Hitler, 1936–1945: Nemesis*, by Ian Kershaw. *Guardian* (London), October 7: 8.
7. Review of *The Third Reich: A New History*, by Michael Burleigh. *National Interest* (Winter): 103–6.

2001

1. Review of *Constantine's Sword: The Church and Jews—A History*, by James Carroll. *Inside the Vatican*, March/April: 50–51.
2. Review of *Lord Acton*, by Roland Hill. *Los Angeles Times Book Review*, April 8: 1.
    a. Translated into Hungarian in *Klió*, no. 3, 2001.
3. Review of *Churchill: A Biography*, by Roy Jenkins; *Churchill: A Study in Greatness*, by Geoffrey Best; and *War Diaries, 1939–1945*, by Field Marshall Lord Alanbrooke. *Los Angeles Times Book Review*, November 18: 1.

4. Review of *The World since 1945: An International History*, by P. M. H. Bell. *National Interest* (Fall): 140–42.
5. Review of *Churchill: A Biography*, by Roy Jenkins. *Spectator* (London), October 13: 48–49.
6. Review of *Huszezeregy Éjszaka*, by Alexander Bródy. *Magyar Hirlap*, November 29.

2002

1. Review of *A Moral Temper: The Letters of Dwight Macdonald*, by Michael Wreszin. *Chronicles*, February: 32–33.
2. Review of *The American Line: 1871–1902*, by William Henry Flayhart. *Pennsylvania History* (Winter): 102–4.
3. Review of *Crowd Culture*, by Bernard Iddings Bell. *University Bookman* (Fall): 5–7.
4. Review of *Alamein*, by Jon Latimer; *Alamein*, by Stephen Bungay; *Alamein: War without Hate*, by John Bierman and Colin Smith; and *An Army at Dawn*, by Rick Atkinson. *Los Angeles Times Book Review*, November 24: 11–12.
5. Review of *Napoleon and Wellington*, by Andrew Roberts. *Los Angeles Times Book Review*, December 22: 8.

2003

1. Review of *The Conquerers*, by Michael Beschloss. *Los Angeles Times Book Review*, January 26: sec. R, 4.
2. Review of *Churchill's Cold War: Politics of Personal Diplomacy*, by Klaus Larres. *New Republic*, January 13: 35–38.
    a. Translated into Hungarian in *Klió*, no. 2: 90–97.
3. Review of *Amsterdam*, by Geert Mak. *Journal of the Historical Society* (Spring): 221–22.
4. Review of *The Culture of Defeat*, by Wolfgang Schivelbusch. *Los Angeles Times Book Review*, August 3: 11.
5. Review of *Pattern and Repertoire in History*, by Bertrand Roehner and Tony Syme. *Historically Speaking*, September: 35–38.
6. Review of *The Hungarians: A Thousand Years of Victory in Defeat*, by Paul Lendvai. *National Interest* (Fall): 125–27.

Part IV: Miscellaneous

1948

1. Letter. *New York Times Magazine*, 12 September: 2.

1949

1. Letter. *New York Times*, 29 April.

1950

1. Study Group Reports, U.S.-U.S.S.R. Relations ("Minority Opinion"). *World Affairs Councilor*, Philadelphia, August: 4–5.

1951

1. "Kremlin's Rulers Not Superhuman When Heat Is On." *Saturday Evening Post*, May 19: 10, 12.

1953

1. Letter. *Commonweal*, September: 539.
2. Contribution to section titled "Critics' Choice for Christmas." *Commonweal*, December 4: 241–42.

1954

1. Letter. *Uj Hungária*, September 17.
2. Letter. *Commonweal*, November 12: 68–69.
3. "An Autumnal Mood." Review of *Melbourne*, by Lord David Cecil. Contribution to section titled "Critics' Choice for Christmas." *Commonweal*, December 10: 293–94.

1955

1. Letter. *U.S. Naval Institute Proceedings*, February: 213.
2. Letter. *Reporter*, February 10: 6.

1956

1. Contribution to the Loyola Toynbee Symposium. *Mid-America*, April: 73.

1957

1. "An Examination of the Correspondence between Alexis de Tocqueville, Arthur de Gobineau, and Nicholas Khanikov." *American Philosophical Society: Year Book 1957.* Summary of Grant no. 1929 (1955): 333–34.
2. Poem: "The French in Cyprus, 1956." *Commentary*, January: 71.

1958

1. Letter. *Commentary*, April: 352.

1959

1. Tocqueville Centenary: Program and Summary. April 13–14: 959.

1961

1. Letter: "Comment on Tocqueville Article." *French Historical Studies* (Spring): 123–25.
2. Letter: "Answering Professor Hook." *East Europe* 10, no. 10 (October): 39, 51. Reply to Sidney Hook's review of *A History of the Cold War*, in *East Europe* 10, no. 8 (August): 19.
3. Contributions to "The Communist Bloc—How United Is It?" and "A Bridge to Freedom," *East Europe* 10, no. 11 (November): 4, 7, 33–34.
4. Letter: "Haffner on Germany." *Encounter*, December: 93–94.

1962

1. Letter. *Encounter*, November: 94.
2. Correspondence. *American Political Science Review*, March: 141–42.

1963

1. "Father Lynch: A Memoir." *Fournier News*, November 20: 3.

1966

1. Letter. *Daily Republican* (Phoenixville, PA), January, sec. A, 4.
2. "Várhatunk-e változást a nemzetközi politikában és Magyarországon 1966–ban?" Roundtable, New York, March 11.
3. Letter. *Daily Republican* (Phoenixville, PA), November 4, sec. A, 4.

1967

1. Letter. *Daily Republican* (Phoenixville, PA), sec. A, 4.

1968

1. Letter: "The Bolsheviks—50 Years After." *New York Times Magazine*, January 7: 112–13.

1969

1. Letter: "Patriot or Nationalist?" *New York Times*, November 9: sec. E, 15.
2. Letter. *LaSalle Collegian*, November 25: 14.

1970

1. Letter. *Commentary*, June: 25.

1973

1. Author-Reviewers symposia: "*The Passing of the Modern Age*." Peter A. Bertocci, Richard L. Morrill—Author's Response, John Lukacs. *Philosophy Forum* 12: 2–14.

1975

1. Interview. *Philadelphia Inquirer*, March 2: sec. H, 8.

1976

1. Letter. *Horizon*, Autumn: 110.
2. Letter. *Commentary*, November: 27–29.
3. Interview. *Today's Post* (King of Prussia, PA), November 2.
4. Interview: "Prophet of the Past." *Washington Post*, December 31: sec. C, 1–2.

1977

1. Christmas book recommendations. *American Spectator*, December: 27–28.

1978

1. "C. A. Macartney." In *Austrian History Yearbook*, vol. 14, by the American Historical Association Conference Group for Central European History, 435–36. New York/Oxford: Berghahn Books.
2. Franco-American Symposium: "Images of the Two Peoples: Visions of France and America." *Mid-America*, April: 5–12.

1980

1. Obituary: "Ross Hoffman, R.I.P." *National Review*, March 7: 268–69.
2. Letter: "Wallenberg and the Jews of Hungary. Keeping Up with Friends Schlesinger and Liberalism." *New York Times Magazine*, May 4: 36.

1982

1. Letter. *American Spectator*, March: 41.
2. Remarks at symposium: "Tokyo Colloquium." Yomiuri Research Institute, Tokyo, September: 63–75. Also in *Daily Yomiuri*, October: 11–15.

1983

1. Interview. *La Nazione* (Florence), November 26.

1984

1. Response to Sniegoski review. *Continuity*, 105–6.
2. Interview. *Schuylkill Bugle* 1: 4.
3. Letter. *Evening Phoenix* (Phoenixville, PA), February 1.
4. Interview. *U.S. News and World Report*, August 13: 70.
5. Letter: "What Makes Our Candidates?" *Harper's*, September: 6–7.
6. "I Wish I'd Been There." *American Heritage*, December: 38.

1985

1. Excerpts from previous writings. *Raleigh (NC) Reporter*, March 2; April 13; May 11, 25; June 8.
2. "The Best Place to Live." *Philadelphia*, April: 144.
3. Contribution to section titled "Guide to Summer Reading." *Philadelphia*, July: 162.
4. Interview. *Kanadai Magyarság*, July 6.
5. Quip. *New Yorker*, August 5: 67.
6. Letter: "We Are Not the World." *National Review*, November 29: 4.

1986

1. "Churchill y Roosevelt." *La Prensa* (Buenos Aires), January 21. Same in *El Universal* (Caracas), January 24; *Tempo* (Lisbon), January 31–February 8; *Lauh-Kunj* (Jamshepdpur), February 8; *Janta* (Mirzapur), January 23; *Bharat-Ratna-Kesatri*, January 29; *Basti-Khi-Awaz*, February 2; *La Estrella de Panama*, January 22; *Adarsh-Bani*, January 25; *Nainpur-Times*, January 27; *Mai-Rastra*, January 24; *RampurKi-Pukar*, January 26; *Madhya-Yug*, Banda, January 23; *Rashtra-Vhin* (Gorakhpur), January 20.
2. "Orwell's Legacy: A Discussion with John Lukacs, Edward Said and Gerald Graff." *Salmagundi* (Spring/Summer): 121–28.
3. "The Intellectual in Power: A Discussion with Conor Cruise O'Brien and John Lukacs." *Salmagundi* (Spring/Summer): 257–66.

1987

1. Letter: "Schlafly's America." *Harper's*, January: 7.
2. Contribution to "Symposium on Humane Socialism and Traditional Conservatism." *New Oxford Review*, October: 8.

1988

1. Contribution to roundtable: "Best and Worst in the Reagan Administration." *Wall Street Journal*, April 6: 25.
2. Interview. *Pittsburgh Tribune-Review*, April 24.
3. "American." In "Most Overrated/Most Underrated" symposium. *American Heritage*, July/August: 58.

1989

1. Conversation with Bill Moyers (televised, 1988). In *A World of Ideas: Conversations with Thoughtful Men and Women about America Today and the Ideas Shaping Our Future*, edited by Bill D. Moyers and Betty Sue Flowers. New York: Doubleday: 434–46. Also paperbound edition, 1989.
2. Letter. *Evening Phoenix* (Phoenixville, PA) April 3: sec. A.
3. Interview. *Philadelphia Inquirer*, April 30: sec. M, 11.
4. Interview. *Philadelphia Catholic Standard and Times*, May 25.

5. Interview: "Neighbors." *Philadelphia Inquirer*, June 4.
6. Summary of remarks at the Second International Conference on International Relations, University of Paris, September 26–30, 1989. *Newsletter of the American Committee on the History of the Second World War*, Autumn: 6–9.
7. Interview. *168 óra*, August 29.
8. "Enough for One Life." *American Heritage*, December: 76.

1990

1. Interview. *Mozgó Világ*, no. 2: 3–7.
2. Letter. *Evening Phoenix* (Phoenixville, PA), January 10: sec. A.
3. Correspondence. *New Oxford Review* (March): 6–8.
4. "Regret and Promise." Contribution to symposium, "Christianity in Sight of the Third Millennium." *Modern Age* (Summer): 165–68.
5. Interview: "Now for an Opposing Point of View." *Philadelphia*, June: 57–60.
6. Contribution to roundtable: "The Pros and Cons of Immigration." *Chronicles*, July: 15–16.
7. Interview. *Chestnut Hill Local* (Philadelphia), December 27.

1991

1. "History of Schuylkill Township." Schuylkill Township Directory (Chester County, PA).
2. "Current Wisdom." Excerpt from "Berlin Letter." *American Spectator*, April: 43.
3. Interview. *Kurir*, May 2.
4. Interview. *168 óra*, June 4.
5. Letter: "Real Differences in Schuylkill." *Evening Phoenix* (Phoenixville, PA), October 31: sec. A.

1992

1. "A Harper's Magazine Dictionary of Words That Don't Exist but Ought to." Contribution to *In a Word*, edited by Jack Hitt, 21. New York: Dell Publishing.
2. "Appreciating John Lukacs," by Robert H. Ferrell. (Includes sentences from an interview.) *Review of Politics* (Spring): 1–8.

3. Contribution to roundtable: "My Favorite Historical Novel." *American Heritage*, October: 94. Pursuant correspondence: December: 8–9.
4. Letter. *American Heritage*, December: 8–9.

1993

1. Foreword to *As I Saw It: The Tragedy of Hungary*, by Géza Lakatos, i–iii. Englewood, NJ: Universe Publishing.
2. Interview. *Europeo* (Milan/Rome), January 29: 27–29.
3. Reply to letter. *New Oxford Review*, January/February: 6–7.
4. Interview. *Morning Call Magazine* (Allentown, PA), May 3.
5. Interview. *Arkansas Democrat-Gazette* (Little Rock, AR), May 30.
6. Interview. *Washington Times: Insight on the News*, July 5: 14–17.
7. Interview. *Philadelphia Inquirer*, August 5.
8. Quoted in On the Scene: "No Tidal Wave," by Donald Kirk. *National Review*, August 9: 26.
9. Interview. *Magyar Nemzet*, October 16.
10. Interview. *168 óra*, October 19.

1994

1. Excerpts from previous writings. *Raleigh (NC) Reporter*, February 26; March 12, 26; April 23; May 7, 21; June 4, 18; July 2, 16, 30; September 24; October 8, 22; November 5, 19; December 3, 17, 31.
2. Interview. *Beszélö*, January 26.
3. Interview. *Magyar Hirlap*, May 14.
4. Interview. *Népszabadság*, June 11.
5. "A Conversation with John Lukacs" and "Tributes to John Lukacs." (Includes tributes by E. Digby Baltzell, Jacques Barzun, and Robert Maddox.) *Pennsylvania History*, July: 271–87.
6. Interview. *Dagens Nyheter*, Stockholm, September 2.
7. Interview. *Het Parool*, Amsterdam, December 3.
8. "Hitler forutsåg kalla kriget." *Svenska Dagbladet*, Stockholm, December 3.

1995

1. Foreword to *Villanova University: 1842–1992*, by David R. Contosta, xiii–xiv. State College, PA: Pennsylvania State University Press.

2. Interview: "Szindbád Phoenixvilleben." In *Csodák pedig vannak. 12 amerikai karrier*, by György Bolgár and Erzsébet Fazekas, 69–81. Budapest: Lettera Works.
3. Interview. *Uj Magyarország*, January 16.
4. Interview. *Magyar Nemzet*, January 17.
5. Excerpts from previous writings. *Raleigh (NC) Reporter*, January 14, 28; February 11.

1996

1. Contribution to roundtable: "The Responsibility of Intellectuals." In *The New Salmagundi Reader*, edited by Robert Boyers and Peggy Boyers, 453ff. Syracuse, NY: Syracuse University Press.
2. "Thassy Jenö. Egy korkép." Introduction to *Veszélyes vidék: visszaemlékezések*, autobiography of Jenö Thassy. Budapest: Pesti Szalon.
3. "The Reader Replies." *American Scholar* (Summer): 478.
4. Interview. *Népszabadság*, June 26.
5. Excerpts from previous writings. *Raleigh (NC) Reporter*, September 10, October 8.
6. Interview. *Népszava*, December 11.
7. Interview. *Magyar Nemzer*, December 21.

1997

1. Introduction to *Sunflower*, by Gyula Krúdy, translated by John Bátki, 5–22. Budapest: Corvina. (Introduction is largely a reprint of an essay that appeared in the *New Yorker*, December 1, 1986.)
2. "Képek és különbözöségeik." In *Magyarország 2000, Magyarország képe a nagyvilágban*, edited by Gyula Keszthelyi, 153–55. Budapest: Osiris.
3. Interview. *Phoenix* (Phoenixville, PA), January 27: sec. A.
4. Obituary: "Recalling the Life of William H. Reeves III." *Phoenix* (Phoenixville, PA), May 16: sec. A.
5. Excerpts from previous writings. *Raleigh (NC) Reporter*, August 23; September 6, 20; October 4, 18; November 1, 15, 29; December 13.

1998

1. "Erösiteni az önbizalmat." In *III. Magyarország 2000*, edited by Attila Komlós, 580–81. Budapest: Pan Press.

2. Interview. *Népszabadság*, January 31.
3. Interview. *Penn History Review* (Spring): 105–8.
4. Interview. *Kurir*, June.
5. Interview. *Szentendre/Castrum*, June 23.
6. Contribution to roundtable: "America: Triumphant or Troubled?" *American Enterprise*, July/August: 63–64.
7. Letter (concerning Gar Alperovitz and Harry Truman). *Los Angeles Times Book Review*, August 23: 10.
8. Interview. *Svenska Dagbladet*, Stockholm, October 25.

1999

1. Interview. *Demokrata*, no. 25.
2. Interview: "Messze még az egyesult Európa." *Magyar Nemzet*, March 13.
3. "Best Mistake (By Accident)." *New York Times Magazine*, April 18: 134–35.
4. "Ideas." In "Most Overrated; Most Underrated" symposium: *American Heritage*, June: 65.
5. Interview: "Isten görbc vonalakkal ir egyenest." *Népszabadság*, June 19.
6. Interview. *Heti Studentexpressz*, June 22.
7. Interview. *Kónyvhét*, July.
8. Contribution to roundtable: "New People, New Century." *Chronicles*, August: 15–16.
9. Letter. *Phoenix* (Phoenixville, PA), August 10: sec. A.
10. Letter: "The Reader Replies: Is the Universe Designed?" *American Scholar* (Fall): 153.
11. Contribution to "Forgotten Treasures: A Symposium." *Los Angeles Times Book Review*, December 26: 5.

2000

1. Introductory essay to *Krúdy's Chronicles: Turn-of-the-Century Hungary in Gyula Krúdy's Journalism*, edited and translated by John Bátki. Budapest: Central European University Press.
2. Interview. *Népszabadság*, Budapest, January 29.
3. Interview: "Judging Pius XII." *Inside the Vatican*, February: 62.
4. Letter: "Let Residents Run the Roads." *Phoenix* (Phoenixville, PA), February 17: sec. A.

5. "Churchill vs. Hitler: The Duel: The Battle of Minds That Changed History." Consultant and partial writer to television program. *BBC Fourth Programme*, May 8.
6. Interview. *Debrecen*, May 31.
7. Interview: "A történelemnek nincs szaknyelve." *Hajdu Bihari Napló*, June 7.
8. Interview: "A tömeqek demokrácaja." *18 6ra*, Budapest, July.
9. Interview: "Vegetables Don't Have a History: A Conversation with Historian John Lukacs," by Donald A. Yerxa and Karl W. Giberson. *Books and Culture*, July/August: 14–15.
10. "Lukacs Speaks at First Curti Lecture." *Badger Herald* (Madison, WI), October 24.
11. Interview: "Nem kerül erös kézbe az amerikai kormányrúd." *Magyar Hirlap*, Budapest, November 13.

2001

1. Aphorisms. In *Huszezeregy éjszaka*, edited by Alexander Brody.
2. "Hitler." In *Encyclopedia Britannica*, 15th rev. ed., vol. 20, 627–29.
3. "1849: Az europai forradalmak kora lezárult." *Petöfi Irodalmi Múszeum*.
4. Interview. *Fides et Historia* (Winter/Spring): 130–36.
5. Interview. *Enterprise*, May 21.
6. Interview. *Heti Válasz*, June 29.
7. Interview. *Népszáva*, July 7.
8. Interview. *Magyar Hirlap*, July 27.
9. "Nézem a hazámat. Beszélgetés John Lukacs (Lukács Janós) Amerikában élö történésszel." *Népszabadság*, August 25.
10. Interview. *Magyar Nemzet*, September 15.
11. Interview: "Lessons in History," by Laura Fording. *Newsweek*. Newsweek Web Exclusive. September 21. http://www.thedailybeast.com/newsweek/2001/09/20/lessons-in-history.html/ (retrieved December 4, 2012).
12. Obituary: "Bán András halálára." *Népszabadság*, October 1.
13. Interview. *Philadelphia Inquirer*, October 7: sec. H, 1, 7.
14. Quoted in "Man of the Hour: How Should a Leader Lead?" in *People Weekly*, by Alex Tresniowski, Mina Biddle, Molly Fahner, et al. November 12: 141ff.
15. "The Structure of History Is Changing." In "This New War" symposium. *American Heritage*, December: 29.

16. Excerpt of lecture at the Hungarian Embassy (October). *Magyar Nemzet*, December 14.

2002

1. "New Insight on Churchill's View of Hungary." *Budapest Sun*, June 13–19.
2. Interview. *Hetek*, June 14.
3. Interview. *Magyar Nemzet*, June 15.
4. Interview. *Népszabadság*, July 6.
5. Quote. *Merriam Webster's Collegiate Dictionary*, 10th edition: 417.
6. Interview. *Prime Time Magazine* (Bucks County, PA), September.
7. Interview. *O Estado de S. Paulo*, October 6.

2003

1. "History in the Democratic Age: Historian John Lukacs Talks with Chairman Bruce Cole." *Humanities* (January/February): 6–9, 49–50.
2. Letter. *New York Times*, April 25: sec. A, 30.
3. "Philosopher." In "Most Overrated/Most Underrated" symposium. *American Heritage*, October: 47.

Permissions

MOST OF THE SELECTIONS in this book previously appeared in other publications. Grateful acknowledgment is made for permission to reprint the pieces here (sometimes in slightly altered form).

"History as Literature" (as "Re-cognition of History as Literature") appeared as chapter 4 of *The Future of History*, by John Lukacs. Copyright © 2011 by John Lukacs. By special permission of Yale University Press. All rights reserved.

"American 'Exceptionalism'" (as "American 'Exceptionalism': Addenda to Alonzo Hamby's Essay") and "A Tocqueville Tide" appeared in *Historically Speaking*, in the September/October 2008 issue and the November/December 2007 issue, respectively. Copyright © by Johns Hopkins University Press. All rights reserved. Reproduced by special permission.

"The Germans' Two Wars: Heisenberg and Bohr" and "The Origins of the Cold War" (as "The Second World War and the Origins of the Cold War") appeared in *The Legacy of the Second World War*, by

John Lukacs, as chapter 5 and chapter 7, respectively. Copyright © 2010 by John Lukacs. By special permission of Yale University Press. All rights reserved.

"Necessary Evil" (as "Necessary Evil: A review of *Churchill, Hitler, and the Unnecessary War: How Britain Lost Its Empire and the West Lost the World*, Patrick J. Buchanan") appeared in the June 2, 2008, issue of the *American Conservative.* Copyright © 2008 by the *American Conservative.* Reproduced by special permission. All rights reserved.

"The Vital Center Did Not Hold" (as "The Vital Center Did Not Hold: Arthur Schlesinger's diaries reveal a blindness to the changing political landscape") appeared in the March 2008 issue of *Harper's Magazine.* Copyright © 2008 by *Harper's Magazine.* All rights reserved. Reproduced by special permission.

"The World Around Me: My Adopted Country" appeared as chapter 3 of *Last Rites*, by John Lukacs. Copyright © 2009 by John Lukacs. By special permission of Yale University Press. All rights reserved.

Index

INTERCOLLEGIATE
STUDIES INSTITUTE
Educating for Liberty